# LIBERATE YOUR PRAYING HEART

*Gary and Sherry,*
*Be encouraged!*
*John W Frye*

JOHN W. FRYE **LIBERATE YOUR PRAYING HEART**

For the Grandchildren

Benjamin, Zachary, Jackson, Trevor,
Lily, Sylvia, Molly, Jacob, Sophia, Sadie

". . . the next generation will know them . . ."
Psalm 78:6

# CONTENTS

**Foreword**    Rev. Dr. Scot McKnight    xi

**Chapter 1**    Your Praying Heart    1

**Chapter 2**    Celebrating the New Covenant    11

**Chapter 3**    Prayer Begins with God    23

**Chapter 4**    The Real Lord's Prayer    37

**Chapter 5**    The Language of Prayer    45

**Chapter 6**    Carving Away the Stone    63

**Chapter 7**    Absorbing the Psalms    75

**Chapter 8**    Never Say Never    87

**Acknowledgments**    93

**Endnotes**    95

# FOREWORD

In this bold book John Frye informs his readers that one by one they are born to pray and are praying far more than they perhaps know. The immediate relief many will feel flows against the guilt-ingrained messages so many have heard: 15 minutes per day, beginning in silence, then praise, then, then, then, and only then petitions for oneself.

I've heard many, including Eugene Peterson say we pray more than we know because our mental life, if but turned slightly toward God, becomes a prayer life. The Psalms are often little more than one's musings, one's wonderings, one's hopes, one's fears, or one's nightmares put into words but directed toward God.

One can read the first fifty or so psalms in our Bible and wonder if David would not qualify as an official, royal whiner. They'd be right, but they'd be mistaken if they didn't actually consider whining to be a form of prayer. Some pastors don't want to hear that sentence, but I believe it. When we complain with even a tilt of our heart toward God we've turned whining and complaining into one of the Bible's best categories: lamenting.

In one of the classics on the pastoral life, George Bernanos reflects on a pastor's prayer life, beginning with his struggle to find a customary prayer life:[1]

Another horrible night, sleep interspersed with evil dreams. It was raining so hard that I couldn't venture into church. Never have I made such efforts to pray, at first calmly and steadily, then with a kind of savage, concentrated violence, till at last, having struggled back into calm with a huge effort, I persisted, almost desperately (desperately! How horrible it sounds!) in a sheer transport of will which set me shuddering with anguish. Yet — nothing.

But he makes progress when he muses further in the face of God:

> I know, of course, that the wish to pray is a prayer in itself, that God can ask no more than that of us.

Many of course think prayer is a mental trick played by the praying person and sanctified by the Bible. Bernanos muses with that thought into the very presence of God with those who have learned that all of life is prayer:

> But alas! We take the psychiatrists' word for it. The unanimous testimony of saints is held as of little or no account. They may all affirm that this kind of deepening of the spirit is unlike any other experience, that instead of showing us more and more of our own complexity it ends in sudden total illumination, opening out upon azure light—they can be dismissed with a few shrugs. Yet when has any man of prayer told us that prayer had failed him?

Christian, be encouraged. Prayer is not just a rigid time spent before a meal or in a disciplined time frame. Turn your thoughts, your worries, your fears and all your complaints toward God and you will join the saints of prayer, who at times had no idea they too were praying.

God is listening.

**Rev. Dr. Scot McKnight**
Julius R. Mantey Professor of New Testament
Northern Seminary
Author, *Praying with the Church*

# one
# YOUR PRAYING HEART

You are a praying person. Does that startle you? Consider it again: you, and I do mean *you*, are a praying person. You don't need to *learn* to pray. You need to be *liberated* to pray. Within the package containing the big, bountiful, free gift called salvation was included a praying heart. Most Christians are unaware of this tremendous gift. That you already have a praying heart is an epic idea. I want to explore this fascinating reality with you. Why? So that you will find prayer to be as vital a part of your life as breathing.

If you are anything like me, you have agreed that prayer is a core practice of being a child of God. You want to pray and pray well. You have heard other people pray, and something inside you says "Yes! That's the way it should be." But it isn't that way in your prayer life. You have read books on prayer. For a while after reading a good book, your prayer life pulsates with new enthusiasm. But not for long. There seems to be no staying power. You feel frustrated; you just know you're letting God and yourself down. Why does it seem so difficult to persistently and passionately engage in something as important as prayer?

To embrace the fact that you are a praying person does not mean that you already pray well or enough. But the crux of the issue is this: you have a praying heart. You are, already, a praying person. *The challenge lies in catching up to what God has already made you to be.*

I am convinced that you have every reason to lie down at night and breathe a sigh of satisfaction. Imagine with me for a moment the Father in heaven whispering over you, "With your prayer life I am well pleased!"

The Jesuit priest Gregory Boyle, who grew up in the gang area of Los Angeles, has for twenty years been working with gang members, offering them an alternative to a life of drugs, sex, violence, and premature death. He has written a book containing stories of the triumphs and tragedies of his ministry to one of the hardest-to-reach people groups. His gracious approach to the Homies and Homegirls has been to offer them jobs; he calls these job opportunities "Home Boy Industries." Father Gregory is known in the 'hood as "G-dog."

On one occasion, while working with a guy called Sharkey, G-dog decided to alter his strategy—to "catch [Sharkey] in the act of doing something right." Gregory was impressed with the result. He told Sharkey that he was heroic, basing his assessment on the young man's courage demonstrated in the significant changes he was making in his life. Gregory asserted that Sharkey's fearlessness greatly surpassed the "bravery" of his violent barrio past, telling him, "You are a giant among men." Starkey, quite unbalanced by this frank affirmation, silently stared at G-dog, finally responding, "G-dog, I'm gonna tattoo that on my heart."[2]

Tattoo on the heart. Sometimes something hits us so deeply that we want to carry it forever. We want it in—and on—our heart. Deep. Permanent, like a tattoo. Here's the truth: God has done a deep, lasting work in you. God has tattooed prayer into your deepest being.

Somewhere in the midst of the many books, countless sermons, and slick techniques on and for prayer we lose sight of the quiet, mysterious, subterranean energies of *the God-given, praying heart.* We received from God a heart oriented toward himself and toward the God-given prayers of the Bible. God creates in us a passion for prayer when he recreates us as new persons in Jesus Christ.

When I first understood this liberating truth I wanted to shout it from the housetops. I have chosen instead to write a book. I'm too old to shout for long.

Take a deep breath and let out a sigh of relief. There's no guilt here—no shame, no sense of failure, no doubt about possibility. The salvation reality is that *you, right now,* are a praying person.

Michelangelo, the great Italian artist and sculptor, wrote, "In every block of marble is an angel. The task of the sculptor is to set it free."[3] In the inner being of every child of God is a vibrant, praying heart. Your task is to liberate it.

I desire to be a friend, our spiritual director, to guide us on this liberating journey. I say "our," not "your," spiritual director because I too am in the process of liberating my praying heart. This is an exhilarating challenge.

You do not need to be prodded, pressured, or guilt-tripped to pray. You may have read books on prayer. I certainly have. When it comes to prayer, we need liberation, not information. Our hearts need to be released, set joyously free to fulfill our calling as God-created, praying persons. Where the Spirit of the Lord is, there is liberty. This is certainly true of your prayer life.

The fact that you are already a praying person does not mean that there is nothing further for you to do. Liberating your praying heart requires what a wise, seasoned mentor once taught me. Dr. Victor Matthews, who taught theology at Grand Rapids Theological Seminary, talked often about "the divine-human cooperative." We are invited by God to be "co-workers" with him to set free our passionate, praying hearts.

The work—from your side—of liberating your praying heart will require patience, determination, and establishing some effective skills. The key reality you and I face as we seek to mature in prayer is not a failure to learn. Our main focus must be on becoming consciously aware of and intentionally joining in with our already God-implanted, praying hearts.

On a crisp Monday morning a group of us participated in a prayer walk around and near our church building. I asked a sweet elderly lady to launch our walk with an opening prayer. Because of her weak legs we placed on the sidewalk in front of the church building a chair for her to sit in on. She balked at my request, and I gently insisted she could do it. She offered up a short, honest prayer to God—absolutely on target for the event that day.

The next day, however, she timorously pulled me aside as she was getting ready to join others in making quilts. "Pastor John, can I talk to you alone for a minute?" We stepped out into the hallway, out of hearing of the others. She nestled in close to me and looked up with a serious face.

Sounding nervous, she confided in me in her sweet North Carolina drawl, "You asked me to pray yesterday morning. I felt so embarrassed. I'm not good at praying with others. I really don't know how. Please don't ask me to do that again."

I assured her that she had done just fine the previous morning, that her prayer had been brief and significant, an excellent launch for the prayer walk. I also apologized for making her feel awkward and assured her that I would not do that to her again, and she thanked me for the reassurance. She was relieved . . . and I was concerned.

If she only knew! She is an amazing pray-er. Yet, sadly, over the years of her life she has picked up many prayer-defeating ideas. If only she could recognize that her new heart is alive and praying ceaselessly to God. Maybe she doesn't believe that, yet it's rock solid true—true for her and true for you.

## THE BASICS

In any discussion about prayer we begin with God. I will repeat this often. Faulty thinking suggests that prayer begins and ends with us. Not true. God created you to be a pray-er.

When God saved you through the merits and mediation of Jesus Christ, he saved you into a vibrant prayer life. Through Christ you are a card-carrying participant in the new creation—and the new creation runs on prayer. The moment Jesus stepped alive from the tomb he began making all things new, *very much including your prayer life*. Prayer begins with God—God the Father, God the Son, and God the Holy Spirit. This is an important, basic truth we will consider repeatedly.

I imagine your insisting, "You're going to have to convince me! I have struggled with prayer for much of my life." As have so many of us. Yet today is a new day, and you are on the verge of an exciting new discovery. For so long when people have heard the word *prayer* they have felt guilty. You might be someone who still complains, "How can you even suggest that I *am* a praying person? I have tried and failed at prayer so many times. Sometimes I wonder if I'll ever be able to pray the way I should." Friend, don't give up.

## THE STRUGGLE

Your struggles with prayer are not unique. Thousands of Christians believe that they do not pray enough or in a manner that will move God to respond. This is not because they devalue prayer; they know it to be a dynamic and crucial reality in the Christian life. The core problem is that so many have bought into the error that prayer begins and ends with them.

Many of our prayer-rockets have been launched from the wrong pad. We roared into the Christian life with excitement and joy, only to find our flight pattern diverted by cautions and stipulations. We were told, in effect, "You *have to* become a praying person. You *have to* learn to pray. You *need* a simple pattern. You *must* learn these crisp, systematic steps for prayer. You *ought to* persist in prayer. You *must* relentlessly practice the discipline of prayer. You *need* this prayer technique." Eugene Peterson, a trusted mentor in spiritual matters, counsels, "Development in prayer does not come through acquired techniques but through growing intimacy with the Father, revealed in Jesus, by the Spirit."[4] We got blasted by a barrage of ought to's, shoulds, have to's, musts, and need to's. In a bewildering, counterintuitive turnaround, all the pressure urging us to pray ended up grounding our prayer lives. With so many well-intentioned directives we begin to wonder, "Are we really free to go against all this well-intentioned pressure to learn to pray and simply pursue an unimpeded praying heart?"

## DISCIPLINE

Many of us break out in hives when we hear the word *discipline*. It's a killer word, especially in our "do-as-you-please" culture. Didn't the restrictions of discipline disappear with eight-track tapes and bell-bottom pants? "The discipline of prayer" is a daunting phrase, as grinding in our minds as the dentist's drill as she addresses a root canal. Avoidance is surely the safest strategy. We have been poisoned into believing a deep, spontaneity-destroying lie: the prayer ball is always in our court. We're just not up to the challenge.

Think about it. Would God do that? Would God leave the responsibility for something as imminently important as prayer totally to our feeble minds and weak wills? My response is a resounding No! This whole approach is wrong. It is my intention to establish that the impetus for and effectiveness of *prayer are first and always in God's court.*

## LORD, TEACH US TO PRAY

What if *liberation* is the key word? Some might raise another objection to the idea—allow me to substitute "truth"—that we have been recreated as praying persons. They might fittingly remind us that Jesus' own disciples entreated the Lord, "Teach us to pray" (Luke 11:1). Their request is relevant and must not be ignored.

The disciples' request, however, does need to be probed. The traditional thinking is framed like this: if Jesus' disciples asked him to teach them to pray, doesn't that mean that we, too, have to *learn* to pray? This is a reasonable question, one that seems to stand in opposition to the main theme of this book—that *we need only to be liberated to pray.*

Because this was one of many strategic moments in the lives of Jesus's disciples, a few observations are pertinent. First, who exactly were these men who asked Jesus to teach them to pray? Don't leap to a hasty conclusion. The disciples were Jewish men who had been raised within the culture of first-century, second Temple Judaism.[5] What was prayer life like for most men in that Jewish culture? The disciples attended synagogue every Sabbath and practiced praying three times a day—morning, mid-afternoon, and evening.

Second, what was the content of the first-century Jewish prayers? These twelve men had grown up routinely praying the psalms and daily offering thanks for food, for health, and for the blessings of life. *Jews in Jesus' world were an obsessively praying people.*

The twelve disciples asking Jesus to teach them to pray could be likened to New York Yankees baseball players asking the now retired Derek Jeter to teach them to play. Professionals asking to be taught the game! How awkward. Many of us might consider Jesus' disciples to have been prayer professionals when compared to our feeble, unstructured, and sporadic prayer lives.

What did it mean, then, for Jesus' disciples to ask for instruction on prayer? The disciples reminded Jesus that John the Baptist taught his disciples to pray. John, Jesus' cousin, had roared onto the scene like a tornado and was even then serving as the agent of a massive repentance revolution in Israel: "And so John the Baptist appeared in the wilderness, preaching a baptism of repentance for the forgiveness of sins. The *whole Judean countryside* and *all the people of Jerusalem* went out to him. Confessing their sins, they were baptized by him in the Jordan River" (Mark 1:4–5, emphasis added). As a prophetic phenomenon with whom the Jewish leaders and people had to reckon, John was not someone to be ignored.

Jesus' disciples were witnesses to their master's own astounding teachings and to his startling displays of divine power. Jesus cast out demons, healed diseases, and calmed stormy seas. The disciples also observed that Jesus was a determined person of prayer: "Jesus often withdrew to solitary places and prayed" (Luke 5:16).

There was something in Jesus' prayer life that caused all that the disciples knew about prayer to seem distressingly inadequate. Jesus held the golden chalice of prayer; in comparison, their repetitive, routine prayers must have seemed like offerings held up in Styrofoam cups. As persistent as their ritualistic prayer schedule was, they seemed to know nothing about the authentic nature of prayer. Thus their request.

## GOD TALKING TO GOD

Press pause. Then ponder this thought: when Jesus prayed, it was a situation of God talking to God. At some mysterious level this observation is true for you as well. As observed by the prayer master P. T. Forsyth, "When we speak to God it is really the God who lives in us speaking through us to Himself."[5] That may be new concept for you. Hold on to it; we will come back to explore this stunning reality.

As Jesus prayed, God was indeed talking to God. What must those prayers have sounded like! I can only imagine that they were permeated with love, driven by passion, reflective of agony and ecstasy, shocking in honesty, stunning in unity, and sparkling with joy.

In Jesus' example we see the prayer life of a new creation person. Jesus was the true man (person)—the authentic human being who prayed, and who continues—continuously—to pray. He prayed the traditional Jewish prayers (the psalms), he interceded for others, he offered praises to the Father, and he communed with the Father in deep agony and with loud weeping. Jesus prayed the whole spectrum of human experience. He prayed to his Father, and when he did so God was dialoguing with God.

I doubt you will disagree that *Jesus was and is a praying person.* Now consider that, as a child of God, you are "in Christ" ("in the Messiah")—a phrase that was among the apostle Paul's favorite expressions, appearing no fewer than 165 times in his 13 letters. The praying Christ (Messiah) is *in* you, just as you are *in* him.

The Christ who is now our life (Colossians 3:1–2) is eternally praying for his church, and because you are a child of God his prayers target you:

> Therefore he [Jesus] is able to save completely those who come to God through him, because *he always lives to intercede for them* (Hebrews 7:25, emphasis added).

Jesus eternally lives to intercede for—that means to pray for—those whom he has saved. You are on Jesus' prayer list. The apostle Paul agrees, asking rhetorically,

> Who then is the one who condemns? No one. *Christ Jesus who died—more than that, who was raised to life—is at the right hand of God and is also interceding for us* (Romans 8:34, emphasis added).

Well, there you have it. As in the TV commercial, I shout "But wait! There's more!" The Holy Spirit is an unceasing pray-er for you too. Again Paul writes,

> In the same way, the Spirit helps us in our weakness. We do not know what we ought to pray for, but *the Spirit himself intercedes for us* through wordless groans. And he who searches our hearts knows the mind of the Spirit, because the Spirit intercedes for God's people in accordance with the will of God" (Romans 8:26–27, emphasis added).

Talk about a prayer team! You have Jesus and the Holy Spirit in your court, both actively praying for you. The point is this: *your praying heart longs for you to join with Jesus and the Holy Spirit in this continuous conversation with the Father.* You are invited to join in the most life- and world-changing, ongoing dialogue in the world.

To explore the origins of our praying hearts we will need to take a trek into some astounding Old Testament passages in which we will discover promises that point toward prayer as a pulsating reality. A reality so valuable to God that God would never leave its operation or effectiveness up to frail, fickle, and fumbling folks like us. When God saves people, God creates pray-ers.

# two

## CELEBRATING THE NEW COVENANT

Just before I wrote this chapter my wife, Julie, and I visited our youngest daughter, Shamar; her husband, Chris; and their eighteen-month-old daughter, Sophia, in San Diego. Sophia is ineffably cute. And she is "talking"—talking a lot, though not yet in recognizable words. It goes without saying that Shamar and Chris have longed for Sophia's first clear words to be "Papa," "Dada," or "Mama."

When we got back home to Grand Rapids, MI, we face-timed with Shamar, who reported that Sophia's first clear word had in fact been "pasta." The family had been eating spaghetti, and so "pasta" had become the word *du jour*. I like to think Sophia was thinking of me, Grandpa—a *pastor*, instead of spaghetti. It could happen . . .

A child's heart is oriented toward "Mama," "Papa," "Grandpa" (and "Grandma")—I had to include that parenthetical addition to guarantee continued welcome in the house. Our praying hearts, too, are oriented toward *"Abba"*—toward Father, or even "Daddy." How did this marvelous God-as-Father orientation ever come about? Good question.

My first big aim in this section is to reframe how you think about prayer. Once you see what God has done and is doing, I suspect your prayer life will never be the same.

## OLD TESTAMENT WEDDING

First, in order for us to grasp the reality that God gives us a praying heart when we become Jesus followers, it will help to examine a few Old Testament passages. Stay with me here; don't let this section bog you down. We're in hot pursuit of an amazing reality. I don't get tired of writing it: *you are a praying person.*

One of the most startling aspects of God's salvation is what Christians call the New Covenant. A quick review of Israel's history will help us appreciate the concept. After Adam and Eve sinned God kicked into gear to save the people of this rebellious planet. After some time God entered into a covenant—an agreement—with Abram (later called Abraham), pledging to make from his descendants a nation that would bless all the nations of the earth (Genesis 12:1–3). Later God met his people, the liberated slaves, at the base of Mount Sinai following their exodus and escape from Egypt, and declared himself to be their God. God was gathering more than a million former slaves and creating from them a mighty nation. In a culture of many gods, Yahweh (the LORD) alone was declaring himself to be Israel's God. The first two of the Ten Commandments nailed this down:

And God spoke all these words:
"I am the LORD your God, who brought you out of Egypt, out of
 the land of slavery.
"You shall have no other gods before me.
"You shall not make for yourself an image in the form of
 anything in heaven
above or on the earth beneath or in the waters below. You shall
 not bow down to
them or worship them."
*(Exodus 20:1–5a)*

The Mosaic Law spelled out the terms of the agreement between God and his people. God likened this covenant to a marriage certificate. God, who would be a faithful husband, was calling Israel to be his faithful wife. God married his bride at Sinai.

The turbulent story of the Old Testament demonstrates again and again that Israel failed miserably as God's Beloved. God was shocked, heartbroken, and angry over Israel's pursuit of idols gods:

> I gave faithless Israel her certificate of divorce and sent her away because of all her adulteries. Yet I saw that her unfaithful sister Judah had no fear; she also went out and committed adultery. Because Israel's immorality mattered so little to her, she defiled the land and committed adultery with stone and wood. In spite of all this, her unfaithful sister Judah did not return to me with all her heart, but only in pretense," declares the LORD.
>
> The LORD said to me, "Faithless Israel is more righteous than unfaithful Judah. Go, proclaim this message towards the north:
>
> 'Return, faithless Israel,' declares the LORD,
> 'I will frown on you no longer,
> for I am faithful,' declares the LORD,
> 'I will not be angry for ever.
> Only acknowledge your guilt—
> you have rebelled against the LORD your God,
> you have scattered your favors to foreign gods
> under every spreading tree,
> and have not obeyed me,'"
> declares the LORD.
>
> "Return, faithless people," declares the LORD, "for I am your husband. I will choose you—one from a town and two from a clan—and bring you to Zion."
> *(Jeremiah 3:8–14)*

As judgment from God for Israel's idolatry, the Northern Kingdom of Israel fell to the extremely violent Assyrians. Israel had shamelessly prostituted herself to other gods, had become an adulterer and was consequently now a slave to a foreign power. The Lord desired that the southern kingdom of Judah learn from Israel's example. Sadly, Judah was blatantly idolatrous as well, worshiping the pagan gods of the surrounding nations. The prophet Jeremiah declared that the Babylonians would become God's arm of judgment against the the people of Judah if they did not repent. As you will notice in the above passage, God used *marriage as the metaphor* for the binding agreement he had made with his people. God had sent away Israel (with a divorce certificate) and would do the same with Judah. God was and still is serious about having a faithful people. These people who had once been slaves in Egypt, who had become God's beautiful wife, were now reduced once again to slavery, first to the Assyrians and later to the Babylonians. It's a sad story.

The old (Mosaic) covenant (think wedding vows) was violated time and again by God's wife, Israel. God dismissed Israel into exile, yet longed for the day when she would return. In the midst of the anguish and devastating consequences of the broken relationship between God and Israel, God promised a *new* covenant. Determined to fulfill his vows to his beloved people, He would not stop pursuing his wayward wife. As a faithful husband, he would do something startling and bold.

I cannot listen to Josh Groban singing "Broken Vow"[7] without thinking about God and his loving heart for his people. Even though they had trampled on his covenant fidelity and fled for other lovers, God longed for their love. Yet he let them go. In the midst of his pain God found a way to live with the "broken vow." In his infinite wisdom God created a whole new way of being married to his sinful people—to people like us.

## JEREMIAH 31

The old covenant (wedding contract) failed miserably. God's people deserted their husband, and God dismissed his wayward wife. Clearly something new was needed. Enter the *new* covenant, a contract described clearly in two Old Testament passages. The first is Jeremiah 31:31–34 (emphasis added):

"The days are coming," declares the LORD,
"when I will make a *new covenant*
with the people of Israel
and with the people of Judah.
It will not be like the covenant
I made with their ancestors
when I took them by the hand
to lead them out of Egypt,
because they broke my covenant,
though I was *a husband* to them,"
declares the LORD.
"This is the covenant I will make with the people of Israel
after that time," declares the LORD.
"I will put my law in their minds
and *write it on their hearts*.
I will be their God,
and they will be my people.
*No longer will they teach* their neighbor,
or say to one another, 'Know the LORD,'
because they will all know me,
from the least of them to the greatest,"
declares the LORD.
"For I will forgive their wickedness
and will remember their sins no more."

Several wonderful features stand out in Jeremiah's vision of the new covenant. First, *God will take the initiative* to make it happen. Israel's roller coaster history reveals that God's people—and that includes us—cannot stay faithful to him without help. Second, the new covenant will be new not just in *time* but also in *kind*. Unlike the old covenant with Moses, which depended on the obedient actions of the people, it will hinge on new and startling workings of God. The new covenant promises that God's law will be written upon the minds and hearts of God's people, not externally on stone tablets, as with the Law of Moses. Third, there will be no need for *teaching* anything: "No longer will they teach . . ." An authentic relationship with God will be birthed based on the initiative of God himself. There will be no requirement for our

**15**

knowing and keeping laws. In order for us to grasp the implications of all of this, it is imperative that we hold it in the forefront of our thinking. This does not imply, however, that there is *no place* for teaching in the Christian life. The New Covenant, a work of the Holy Spirit based on Jesus' redeeming work accomplished on the cross, will bind God to his people forever.

## EZEKIEL 36

When God says something once, that should be enough for us. Yet the New Covenant is such an amazing act on God's part that he uses another Old Testament prophet, Ezekiel, to reinforce its significance:

> For I will take you out of the nations; I will gather you from all the countries and bring you back into your own land. I will sprinkle clean water on you, and you will be clean; I will cleanse you from all your impurities and *from all your idols. I will give you a new heart and put a new spirit in you*; I will remove from you your heart of stone and give you a heart of flesh. And *I will put my Spirit in you* and move you to follow my decrees and be careful to keep my laws. Then you will live in the land I gave your ancestors; you will be my people, and I will be your God.
> *(Ezekiel 36:24–28, emphasis added)*

The similarities between the two passages are obvious. God's people will be cleansed, receive *a new heart*, receive God's very Spirit, and be transformed from the inside out. God will do spiritual cardiac surgery on his people to keep them faithful. The image of the *heart of stone* juxtaposed against a heart of flesh constitutes a quick glance backward at the old covenant *stone tablets* (Exodus 34:1, 4), whose stipulations Israel incessantly disobeyed. The persistent pull into idolatry that plagued Old Testament Israel will be overcome by God in the new covenant. When the Spirit comes, prayer is going to break out. The prophet Zechariah foresaw this marvelous event:

And I will pour out on the house of David and the inhabitants of Jerusalem *a Spirit of grace and supplication*. They will look on me, the one they have pierced, and they will mourn for him as one mourns for an only child, and grieve bitterly for him as one grieves for a firstborn son.
*(Zechariah 12:10, emphasis added)*

## JESUS AND THE APOSTLES

Fast forward to Jesus, the Messiah (the Christ). Jesus came as Messiah to put the new covenant into operation. He did this through his redemptive death, burial, and resurrection. With his wondering disciples in the upper room during his final Passover, Jesus declared, "This cup is the *new covenant* in my blood, which is poured out for you" (Luke 22:20, emphasis added). These men were Jews who well knew the promises of God recorded in Jeremiah and Ezekiel. Can you imagine their amazement and envision their startled reaction? Can you overhear them mumbling "How can this be? Can our Master be tampering with—actually *changing*—the meaning of the holy Passover meal?"

The apostle Paul emerged as a robust voice announcing the transforming power of the new covenant in the lives of God's people, writing:

> Are we beginning to commend ourselves again? Or do we need, like some people, letters of recommendation to you or from you? You yourselves are our letter, written on our hearts, known and read by everyone. You show that *you are a letter from Christ*, the result of our ministry, written not with ink but *with the Spirit of the living God*, not on tablets of stone but *on tablets of human hearts*. He has made us competent as ministers of a *new covenant*—not of the letter but of the Spirit; for the letter kills, but the Spirit gives life.
> *(2 Corinthians 3:1–3, emphasis added)*

There can be no denying that Paul had Jeremiah's and Ezekiel's prophesies in his mind and heart. And Paul foresaw those prophesies being fulfilled in us—in you. The Old Testament came to a sharp focus in Jesus Christ, resulting in a radical alteration, a reordering and redirection, that continues on in the church and, consequently, in us.

The author of the Book of Hebrews writes expansively and excitedly about Jesus and the new covenant (Hebrews 8–9). In summary,

> For this reason Christ is the mediator of a *new covenant*, that those who are called may receive the promised eternal inheritance—now that he has died as a ransom to set them free from the sins committed under the first covenant.
> *(Hebrews 9:15, emphasis added)*

By Jesus' sacrifice on the cross and the shedding of his blood, as the Lord's table reminds us, the new covenant is dynamically at work in God's people, the church.

I am thrilled about the promise of God, a prominent feature of the new covenant, to give us new hearts. Jeremiah declared, in fact, that God's Word will be written (indelibly and eternally imprinted, like a tattoo) on transplanted human hearts—on stony, unresponsive hearts that have been replaced with fleshy, warm, and responsive hearts. Further, God promises to implant his own Spirit within us to prompt and energize those new hearts.

Paul saw these realities come to life in the Corinthian believers. When he preached "Christ crucified," pagans were transformed into God's family members. The exalted Jesus was calling out his new bride, the church.

The inner lives of God's people have been altered; divine surgery has been performed; and revitalized hearts now beat in place of the old, stony ones. The Spirit who was poured out at Pentecost and who activates the new covenant in our experience is called in Zechariah 12:10 *the Spirit of supplication*, the Spirit of prayer (Zechariah 12:10). The word "supplication," or prayer, in the Hebrew literally means "seeking for grace."[8] Just as the Holy Spirit is the Spirit of truth, of life, and of holiness, so the friendly third Person of the holy Trinity is the Spirit of prayer! A grace-seeking Spirit has been given to you; this Spirit now lives forever in you.

## NEW HEARTS ARE PRAYING HEARTS

It is essential, once again, that we not overlook one vital reality of our new hearts: they are *praying* hearts. Your new heart is oriented toward God the Father, calibrated to continuously seek God. Twice in the New Testament when Paul is describing our relationship to God as God's children, he writes that the Spirit prompts us to address God as "*Abba*, Father":

> The Spirit you received does not make you slaves, so that you live in fear again; rather, the Spirit you received brought about your adoption to sonship. And by him we cry, "*Abba,* Father." (Romans 8:15)

And again,

> Because you are his sons, God sent the Spirit of his Son into our hearts, the Spirit who calls out, "*Abba*, Father." (Galatians 4:6)

Just as Shamar and Chris hoped that Sophia's first clear word would be "Mama" or "Papa," so the Spirit prompts our first words toward God. The new covenant makes us new people in a new and revitalized relationship with God. As God's daughters and sons we cry, "*Abba,*" "Daddy," "Papa," "Father"—terms of affection and love, in the foundational language of love, trust, and hope. Too bad Sophia said "pasta" (that is, "Grandpa") first . . .

## THE STARTLING PROMPT

Sometimes our heart speaks to our mind. Call it intuition. Call it a "hunch." We sense ourselves compelled to make a phone call, face a character flaw, visit a friend, or pull over and pray. I remember being prompted to ask a young wife and mother who was in desperate agony about the condition of her marriage whether she had ever made a decision on an airplane. *Where did that come from?* I wondered. In response, she began to sob and replied, "I was on a plane leaving Africa and I felt like I was deserting God's will for my life. God is judging that decision in my marriage." She went on to explain her feeling that the troubles in her marriage and family were a direct result of her decision to leave mission work in Africa. I was able to assure her that God the Father is not like that. He would not take "revenge" on her by holding an old decision against her. She wept with hope.

Our new hearts are oriented toward God, and the Spirit often nudges them with a question, a memory, or a verse from Scripture. We catch a glimpse of this degree of love and attachment to God in the words of King David: "My heart says of you 'Seek his face!' Your face, LORD, I will seek" (Psalm 27:8).

Did you notice it? What prompted David to declare "I will seek Your face, LORD"? His heart—his praying heart. Something deep within David prodded him: "There's more you need. You need God's face!" The fascinating truth is that the Spirit-empowered heart is oriented toward and does seek God's face. The word "face" in this Old Testament verse is a metaphor for God's loving, ever-attentive presence. You have heard, perhaps, of a heat-seeking missile. We've been given a God's-face-seeking heart! What is unknown to the Spirit? Nothing! The Spirit can direct us in the most casual of settings to help people make eternal discoveries.

## THE CHALLENGE

Your heart is forever urging you to "seek God's face" and crying out "*Abba*, Father." The Spirit in you is a praying Spirit, an interceding Person. The challenge for all of us is to become *more aware* of our new heart condition and passion. What is persistently real in our hearts must be consistently *attended to* in our heads. Our praying hearts must somehow move to the "front burner" of our minds.

The error that has plagued so many for so long is viewing prayer as first of all a head thing. We're exhorted to "learn to pray!"—to pray the right way with right words. To pray according to someone else's artificial formula. It's all head stuff.

Don't get me wrong at this point. I am not belittling serious thought or logical, rational processes; nor am I elevating emotion or sloppy thinking. Still, prayer is preeminently a heart reality. Richard Foster, quoting Jean-Nicholas Grou, writes, "It is the heart that prays, it is to the voice of the heart that God listens and it is the heart that he answers."⁹ Another prayer master wrote, "For the heart is already in a state of prayer. . . . [God the Spirit] takes our heart in tow and turns it toward God. . . . *We are deaf to our praying hearts* . . . we fail to see the light in which we live"¹⁰ (emphasis added).

The stifling case of marble around our vibrant, praying hearts must be chipped or carved away. From blocks of marble Michelangelo liberated angels, and we must go about the process of chiseling away the stony impediments within us that restrict us from full intimacy with the Father. Christ's sacrifice has freed us from bondage to sin. Yes, and yet, we are invited to cooperate with God in liberating our hearts for maximum, unrestrained fellowship with him.

This is not easy, but it is so necessary. The impediments stifling our praying heart may be wrong thinking, either about God or about ourselves. Perhaps bad habits undermine our yearning to pray, or life's hurts have paralyzed our soul. Whatever it is, to carve away our rock casing will be neither comfortable nor painless. Yet it will lead to the glorious process of liberation. Before we face the challenge we need to return to and expand upon one fundamental truth; the music of praying hearts beats to this steady tempo: prayer begins with God.

# three

## PRAYER BEGINS WITH GOD

When I was in junior high school someone gave me a copy of A. W. Tozer's *The Pursuit of God*. As a new Christian I was thrown into the deep end of the pool of devotional literature. A person, however, has to grow into the spiritual depths of someone like A. W. Tozer, to mature in Christ before fully grasping Tozer's passion for God. Tozer was a pastor, a self-taught scholar, and a Christian mystic whose writing and sermons delighted and jolted many souls. As I got older I learned, sadly, that Tozer was a neglectful husband and an absent father. Even some, if not all, very godly people have flaws.

I don't regret the plunge. Tozer's books were ahead of their time, predicting the shallow, me-centered evangelicalism that has dominated the American church since the 1980s. In his classic book *The Knowledge of the Holy—The Attributes of God: Their Meaning in the Christian Life* Tozer stops us cold with his opening sentence: "What comes into our minds when we think about God is the most important thing about us."[11] A few sentences later Tozer follows up with this startling reality: "We tend by a secret law of the soul to move toward our mental image of God."[12]

23

The troubling reality is that we go on to *become like* the vision we've conjured up of the God we worship.

It's important for us to probe the depths of the reality that prayer begins with God. Our mental image of God is foundational if we are to experience a vibrant, consistent prayer life. A charming mechanical bunny beating a bass drum crosses our TV screen. Affectionately known as "the Energizer bunny," it hawks long-lasting batteries superior to those offered by the competition. What is it that infuses our prayer lives with long-lasting energy? I think A. W. Tozer would answer our vision of God.

Sitting across the restaurant table from me was a young man interested in the Christian faith. We were having lunch, and I was there to answer any of his questions about the Christian faith. As an unchurched person, he wasn't sure whether or not he was or even wanted to be a child of God. Beyond that concern, Christianity had become distasteful to him. As we continued in a fairly amiable conversation, I asked him, "What comes to mind when you think about God?"

The young man crossed his arms tightly over his chest in a gesture of defiance and responded with a scowl: "I see an angry face, a look that says, 'You'll never be worthy of Me.' God is unapproachable and condemning. He is unaccepting of me." The young man's words revealed a deeply entrenched cynicism. Given his personal image of God, is it any wonder he had a less than pleasing view of the Christian faith? We can also wonder what his prayer life must have been like, if he had one at all.

## GOD IS FIRST

When it comes to prayer, God is first. God is primary and preeminent. As such, he speaks first. Prayer is and always will be *answering speech*. Eugene H. Peterson writes, "[P]rayer is never the first word, it is always the second word. God has the first word. Prayer is answering speech; it is not primarily 'address' but 'response.'"[13]

Peterson reminds us, also, that those who collected and arranged the books of our Old Testament did so with structural intentionality[14] that served a spiritual purpose. This is notably true in the arrangement of the books of Psalms.

Have you paid attention to the structure of this book? If not, stop here and open your Bible to Psalm 1. Before the beginning of the actual psalm you'll notice a heading titled *Book One*. There are 150 psalms, compiled and arranged into five books. Locate each one in your Bible: Book 1 (Psalms 1–41), Book 2 (Psalms 42–72), Book 3 (Psalms 73–89), Book 4 (Psalms 90–106), and Book 5 (Psalms 107–150).

Each "book" of the Psalms ends in a special way. The last verses of each are called a liturgical formula—a formal and worshipful ending, as follows:

BOOK 1:
Praise be to the LORD, the God of Israel
from everlasting to everlasting.
Amen and Amen.
*(Psalm 41:13)*

BOOK 2:
Praise be to the LORD God, the God of Israel,
who alone does marvelous deeds.
Praise be to his glorious name forever;
may the whole earth be filled with his glory.
Amen and Amen.
This concludes the prayers of David son of Jesse.
*(Psalm 72:18–20)*

BOOK 3:
Praise be to the LORD forever!
Amen and Amen.
*(Psalm 89:52)*

BOOK 4:
Praise be to the LORD, the God of Israel,
from everlasting to everlasting.
Let all the people say, "Amen!"

Praise the LORD.
*(Psalm 106:48)*

BOOK 5:

Psalm 150 in its entirety is the liturgical conclusion to Book 5. Beyond that, Psalm 150 serves as the conclusion to the whole collection of psalms (all five books).

## FIVE TO FIVE

Do you recall another section of the Old Testament that is also a famous set of five books? The first five books of the Old Testament are called Torah, meaning the Law of Moses—sometimes referred to as the Pentateuch (meaning "five volumes").

Jewish scholars and faithful rabbis believed that God had said all he wanted to say in Torah: the books of Genesis, Exodus, Leviticus, Numbers, and Deuteronomy. The rest of the Old Testament, according to this outlook, shows the outworking of Torah in Israel's history. In this paradigm the psalms represent human responses to God's initial creative and commanding word.[15] God spoke first, and humans answer in praise, prayers, and discerning wisdom (the Writings). The Jewish Bible is arranged in three parts: the Law (Torah), the Prophets (including the history books like Judges, 1 and 2 Samuel, Nehemiah, and Esther), and the Writings (the poetic books, including Psalms).

## THE PSALMS

The psalms are human responses to God's Word. As expressed by C. Hassell Bullock, "The Psalms represent the voice of 'everyman.'"[16] These expressions are not intended, primarily or exclusively, for priests and nuns, pastors and monks. The psalms were written for all of Israel, for the whole church, for you. God gave them, since God is first. We are second. So five books of prayers (psalms) answer God's five books of revelation and covenant (Torah). God has spoken, and we respond.

A clarifying note: there is no artificial one-on-one correspondence between the five books of the Law and the five books of

Psalms. In other words, Book One of the Psalms is not intended to respond specifically to Genesis, the first book of the Law, nor does Book Two exactly correspond to the content of Exodus, and so on.

Hold up your right hand—one hand, five fingers. That represents God speaking. Revelation. Now place your left hand against your right hand, palms touching. This hand represents our prayers to God. Response. Your hands are now in the classic gesture of prayer. (If you've lost a finger or hand, forgive me for the discrepancy in this simple illustration.)

## A WRONG VIEW OF GOD

The tragic story of Israel is that by the time Jesus came Israel's vision of God had degenerated. Their God, who had purposed to bless the nations of the world through his people (Genesis 12:1–3), had become in their mind a God who played favorites and wanted to curse every other nation except Israel. Even within Israel in the time of Jesus various factions of Judaism viewed themselves as God's favorites. Some of the well-known parties were the Sadducees, Pharisees, Essenes, Herodians, and Zealots. Israel construed God as a great Power they nonetheless needed to protect until he had unleashed destructive judgment on all non-Jewish peoples. Notions of how God was to be protected and Israel to be preserved differed radically among these entrenched factions.

By the time of Jesus the popular expectation was that a militant, mighty Messianic King would arrive and smack down the pagan nations, especially Israel-occupying Rome. When Rome said "peace," the unspoken meaning was "the power of the sword." When Messiah came, Gentile nations would be squashed into submission and God would restore Israel to the top of the heap, over the conquered peoples. Their God would come to their aid as a mighty, conquering King! Hosanna! Israel would be the Queen of the nations.

Jesus' disciples and the Jewish crowds wondered if—and even expected that—a genuine holy war would break out in Jerusalem during Passover week. God would smite the enemy, resulting in a glorious victory that would usher in an exodus from Roman imperial bondage and a vindication of Israel and of Israel's God before the conquered nations.

That divine smack-down didn't happen at the time of the "triumphal entry." The same fickle crowds jubilantly shouting "Hosanna!" would instead be bellowing "Crucify him!" just a few days later. (It is Palm Sunday as I write these sentences.)

One of the primary reasons Jesus came was to reveal the true character of the Old Testament God. Jesus had to confront, resist, and rewire his disciples' and Israel's distorted views of God.

Paul and the other apostles also had to announce the character of the true God to a polytheistic Roman Empire devoted to a multitude of capricious idols. The banner slogan of the early church was "Jesus is Lord"—not Caesar or any other of the thousands of pagan deities. "Therefore," asserts Paul, "I tell you that no one speaking by the Spirit of God says, 'Jesus be cursed,' and no one can say 'Jesus is Lord,' except by the Spirit" (1 Corinthians 12:3).

Contemporary American culture is becoming more and more like that of the first-century world in terms of peoples' views of God/gods.[17] The cultural issues we face include pluralism, intensified racism, post-modernism, materialism, and globalism, not to mention that the fundamentalist militancy in many religions of the world is causing great concern. We inhabit a religiously fractured planet, as well as a politically broken and racially hostile one.

I remember seeing a well-dressed businessman in Mumbai, India, lying prostrate on a colorful tiled floor before an idol, a god with a human form and the head of an elephant. He was asking this god of prosperity to bless his business endeavors. Indeed, when we say the word "god" in our world we may have no real idea what is coming to mind for the person(s) we are addressing. For those of us in the United States, only the names of the idols may be different from those in Jesus' day or from those of India. Yet they are idols just the same; among them are greed, power, money, pleasure, and security. It's essential that we not lose touch with A. W. Tozer's claim: what comes to our minds when we think of God is the most important thing about us.

## PERICHORESIS

The Christian heart yearns for the true God. Our hearts long to be in communion with the God expressly revealed in the teachings and life of Jesus, the Christ. In particular, the believing heart seeks God, the Three-in-One: the trinitarian God revealed in the Bible.

What comes to your mind when you think "God"? Train yourself to think beyond God the Father, to incorporate Trinity as intrinsic to your conception of God. Most of us as Christians do think of Father, Son, and Holy Spirit. This is good, but it is just a start. *Prayer is most effectively engaged when we understand (as much as is humanly possible) how Father, Son, and Spirit relate to one another.* An ancient word that is finding new traction among many Christians in the Protestant stream is *perichoresis.* The word has been appreciated for centuries in the Catholic and Eastern Orthodox traditions.

*Perichoresis* is often translated (wrongly, according to some) as "circle dance." Another common term is "rotation," and some suggest the idea of "making room for another."[18] The word was coined as a genuine attempt to apprehend and appreciate the inner workings of the Trinity.

The simple question *perichoresis* tries to answer is this: How do the persons of the Trinity relate to one another? There can be no doubt that this question brings us face-to-face with a profound mystery. We are on the holiest of ground when trying to know and understand God "on the inside," so to speak. Is it possible for us, finite and limited creatures that we are, to comprehend any of this?

Dennis F. Kinlaw thinks we can. He writes, "Jesus insists that he is a window on the inner life of God himself, not on just how God relates to his world. Later the church fathers used two phrases to express this. They spoke of seeing God 'from the outside' (*ab extra*) and 'from the inside' (*ab intra*). We as creatures only see him from the outside. Jesus' claim is that he knows and sees God from the inside."[19] Many of Jesus' sayings in the Gospel of John invite us to catch a sneak peek into that most eternal and primal knowledge. God the Son—God in human flesh—offers us a preliminary glimpse into the inner relational dynamics of Father, Son, and Spirit.

Again, the word *perichoresis* was coined as a human attempt to describe the relational dynamics among Father, Son, and Holy Spirit. The Person and event of Jesus of Nazareth claiming to be Israel's God caused the early Church Fathers to struggle with regard to their definitions of the Father, the Son, and the Holy Spirit and with regard to their respective claims to deity. These three Persons, they understood, are not three Gods but one. The word *Trinity* was also introduced into orthodox terminology in an attempt to capture this essential reality.

Some proponents denied that Jesus was God on an equal footing with the Father,[20] while others denied that the Holy Spirit was God.[21] They considered the Spirit to be not a Person but a holy influence or force. These varied faulty views about the Godhead can be traced to a teacher named Arius. Against these competing views, the Church Fathers hammered out and defended what is today considered trinitarian orthodoxy.

*Perichoresis* describes a dynamic, loving, joyful, unified vision of the interrelationships among Father, Son, and Holy Spirit— the amazing mutuality and glorious harmony within the godhead. The Trinity does not operate on the "top down" model of a command-and-control relationship, where God the Father is the "boss" and the Son and Spirit exist only to do his bidding. *Perichoresis* seeks to explain how the "one God in three Persons" operates mutually in creating, sustaining, loving, and redeeming the entire cosmos. The concepts of "circle dance" and "making room for another" function as metaphors or picture words.

Think of the three Persons of the Trinity as being eternally alive in an unbreakable, dynamic relationship. Rather than residing in "separate rooms" of Being, so to speak, the three Persons are forever interpenetrating, invading, dancing into each other's

Being—into one another's rooms. The Trinity is a matrix of the vibrant *life* of three Beings circling, rotating, and relating with—and within—one another. There is no eternal hierarchy or rank in God but everlasting, mutual participation in Being God, the three-in-one. As God—the Father, Son, and Holy Spirit are fully equal in both essence (being) and function (doing). This does not mean the Father and the Spirit died on the cross. Only Jesus did. It does mean, however, that there was a mysterious participation of the Three Persons in the redemptive suffering.

What do those inner relational dynamics of the Trinity look like? This is again an excursion into mystery that early Church Fathers sought to understand and explain. The challenge they faced was how the one God of Israel could exist as God the Father and also as Jesus the Son. Even the reality of the deity of the Holy Spirit became a dispute about the relationships of and within the Trinity.

A related question was this: If Jesus was at the same time both God and a human being, how did his divine nature, his deity, relate to his human nature, his humanity? Was Jesus in fact two persons? If so, did he then have two wills? How, and when, did the Holy Spirit become viewed as a Person? We owe God a debt of thanks for the early church definers and defenders of Christian truth. Let us be grateful for their faith, diligence, and persistence in identifying and expressing the tenets of the orthodox faith.

A recognized and respected New Testament scholar is Gordon D. Fee. I have worked my way through his commentary on 1 Corinthians and have not only been taught but also blessed. Another book by this author, *God's Empowering Presence: The Holy Spirit in the Letters of Paul*, considers every reference to the Spirit/spirit in Paul's New Testament writings. I was intrigued by the following quote, which speaks to the inner relationships within the Trinity. Fee writes,

> Here is certain evidence that the Spirit is at once both fully God, as a constituent part of divine reality, and distinct from the Father. On the one hand, the closest kind of intimate, interior

relationship exists between the Father and the Spirit, so close that the only proper analogy for it is the human spirit, as the interior expression of personality. As with Christ in the creed, the Spirit is God of very God. To put this in experiential terms, in our reception of the Spirit, we are on intimate terms with none other than God himself, personally and powerfully present, as the one who in this case reveals God's ways to us. But that at the same time the Spirit is not identical with the Father. The Spirit, as a distinct personality, alone knows—and reveals to us—God's thoughts, God's ways. In the same way Paul will assert in Rom[ans] 8:27 that the Father has the same intimate knowledge of the Spirit. Distinct, they nonetheless function as one.[22]

That is the *perichoretic* dynamic!

An ancient icon (in this case a painting)[23] sought to capture the *perichoresis* (see page 33). I am by no means a scholar of icons, but as I ponder the image I see these things. The icon depicts three persons (symbolic of Father, Son, and Spirit) sitting in a circle at a table. No hierarchy. There is a sense of mutual holiness, in that each sits under a nimbus, a halo. Each person has his head bent—a picture of deferring to one another in love. They are "at table," enjoying communion or fellowship. Bright, yet different, colors illustrate each of the three distinct persons. Their facial features are identical, suggesting that they, together, constitute one God. In some similar depictions connoting the same reality each of the three persons is holding up two fingers in the early church sign of blessing. The persons of the Trinity are blessing one another.

Another visual aid to help us picture the *perichoresis* is this interlocking set of curved lines with a circle:[24]

Imagine the lines and circle in the design pulsating with the dynamic, powerful, eternal life of God, the three-in-one. We see here a depiction of the Trinity, of each of the three Persons interacting or interlocking with the other two, creating spheres of interpenetrating Being. Imagine these Beings dynamically moving (rotating) in and out of one another's spheres—the eternal, elaborately choreographed "circle dance." What the Father does the Son and Spirit also do. What the Son does the Father and Spirit do. And what the Spirit does the Father and Son flawlessly emulate. Eternally, joyfully, lovingly, and in seamless synchrony.

A good illustration of *perichoresis* appears in the 1997 movie *Contact*, in which Jodi Foster plays the character Dr. Eleanor "Ellie" Arroway, a scientist in SETI—an organization dedicated to a search for extraterrestrial intelligence. Ellie is determined to detect signals from space sent by ETs (extraterrestrials). An ET— think beyond the Steven Spielberg character is the movie *ET*— does make contact with Earth, and specifically with Ellie. The ET, within an intricate scheme of codes, sends detailed blueprints to build a machine that will allow Ellie to explore the galaxies of the universe.

Government agents, engineers, and scientists collaborate to construct the machine, a massive structure composed of gigantic, rotating circles of metal. In operation it looks like a giant, whirling gyroscope. The precision, the rotating fury, and the complex unity of so many intricate parts melding into one ball of blazing light combine to constitute a wonder to behold. Imagine this as a possible illustration of the *perichoresis*.

When the machine from an ET intelligence in space reaches a certain speed, with the circles rotating so fast they look like a giant ball of pure energy, Ellie's tiny space pod drops through the middle of it. From within this special space—dare I suggest sacred space?—she is propelled into the dimension of a reality beyond time. And from within that new dimension she is treated to an indescribably beautiful tour of the universe. "They should have sent a poet," she whispers at one point as she gazes upon the startling wonder and staggering beauty before her purview.

She meets her deceased father, who has passed along to her a love for astronomy, on a captivating beach of sand that seems to depict Paradise.

Upon her return from this startling excursion, Ellie is confronted with a shocking "truth"— the whole scientific endeavor has been a failure. She has never actually launched. Video footage shows that the pod had within mere seconds fallen through the core of swirling circles into the churning ocean beneath. According to hard scientific data, Ellie was never launched on a mind-boggling galactic exploration.

The plot thickens: hard science now confronts human experience. Dr. Arroway (Ellie) has reported what she had seen. But she is believed neither by her peers nor by a US government investigative panel.

Matthew McConaughey plays the character of Rev. Dr. Palmer Joss, a renowned Christian philosopher. He sees the dilemma Ellie faces and seeks to assure her that faith does indeed usher people into another dimension of reality. Religion and science are in this instance apparently locking horns. Yet faith is a doorway into reality just as much as science is. Indeed, the point is that faith and science can be allies.

I won't spoil the ending by reciting the scientific data that vindicates Ellie's experience. Here is the significant lesson from the film. The eternal *perichoretic* conversation among Father, Son, and Spirit does indeed invite us to enter an eternal, breath-taking dimension of reality that can be realized only through faith that is expressed in the simple practice of prayer.

Through *perichoresis*, the interpenetrating of the three God-Persons, I believe that we are invited into a realm of dynamic life in which time and eternity blend. As N. T. Wright suggests, our time intersects with God's eternity, our space enters God's sacred "space," and our matter (physicality) gets invited into supernatural joy and transformation.[25]

How can this be? And where do we discover direction to so much as begin to probe these mysterious inner workings of the Trinity? Is all of this mere speculation? Are we treading on sacred ground where we have no right to be?

How do you view yourself before God in prayer? When you pray, are you talking up to an authoritarian God who is all about command and control? Do you feel comfortable, at ease, as though you can relax and be yourself? Or are there holy protocols you dare not mess up? Is it okay for you to pray to the Holy Spirit?

You might respond to that last question with "Come on, John. *Really?*" Yes, really. I had a conversation with a person wringing their hands over whether it was permissable to speak directly to the Spirit. Would it upset the Father and the Son if we were to bypass them in favor of the lowly Holy Spirit?

What if prayer is not about talking up to God-authorities— Father, Son, and Spirit—but about being drawn into a vibrant, joyful, and reciprocal dialogue with them? In this radically new and exciting paradigm of the nature of prayer, the eternal, pulsating, joyful dynamics of the holy Trinity propel us into intimacy, during which we mostly listen. When we do speak our words are weighted with eternity. That is indeed the very life and longing of your praying heart.

I am using the concept of *perichoresis* simply as an illustration pointing to the kind of communication going on within the Trinity into which we are invited. We may gain knowledge from Jesus himself as we listen to the way he describes his life and relationship with his Father. As I have noted, the Gospel of John is a goldmine of insight into that one-of-a-kind relationship. When Jesus prays we observe God conversing with God. In John 17 we catch a glimpse into the continuously relating Being of God, the three-in-one. John 17 is titled "Jesus' Farewell Prayer." That is the topic of the next chapter.

# THE REAL LORD'S PRAYER

A man in my church named Rich suffered from heart issues and was in his final days on earth. When I went to visit him I found in his hospital room a knot of family members huddled in a corner, talking quietly. I leaned over Rich's bed and asked whether he was afraid. In response to his indication that he was not, I asked why that was so. Rich replied simply, "Well, I've never died before." I laughed, as did his family members who were listening in. Even at death's door Rich displayed a faith-driven sense of humor.

## JOHN 17

Jesus, hours from death's door, was surrounded by his closest friends in an upper room in Jerusalem. Sharing his final meal with them, he encouraged them about their future. In fact, an undercurrent of joy characterized Jesus' last hours with his disciples. Jesus also prayed—for himself, for his disciples, and for all believers down through the ages. In that amazing prayer of Jesus we're permitted a glimpse into the beautiful harmony among

Father, Son, and Spirit. Specifically, we can discover in John 17 four inner dynamics of the Trinitarian Being. A fifth dynamic can be discerned in the act of prayer itself. The relational dynamics are:

**unity**, verses 20–23;
**love**, verses 23, 26;
**glory**, verse 24;
**joy**, verse 13 (see 16:22–23); and
**communication** (Jesus prayed to the Father).

A book could be written about each of these captivating realities. The inner workings of the holy Trinity are worth our earnest pursuit, even though we feel ourselves obliged to take off our shoes and whisper "We are on holy ground." Here we will briefly consider each wonderful dynamic.

**UNITY.** Unity, or oneness, in the Trinity means that there is no division or friction among its members. The will of God is eternally cohesive among the three Persons. While eternally distinct as Father, Son, and Holy Spirit, they are indivisibly one not only in essence (being) but also in will (action). The will of the Father is the will of the Son, and the will of the Son corresponds to the will of the Spirit. Listen to Jesus' words to his Father: "My prayer is not for them alone. I pray also for those who will believe in me through their message, *that all of them may be one*, Father, just as you are in me and I am in you. May they also be in us so that the world may believe that you have sent me. I have given them the glory that you gave me, *that they may be one as we are one*—I in them and you in me—so that they may be brought to *complete unity*. Then the world will know that you sent me and have loved them even as you have loved me" (John 17:20–23, emphasis added).

**LOVE.** Love saturates each moment of the eternally consistent interrelationships within the Trinity. This love is more than just admiration and devotion. It is an eternal self-giving of each one to each of the others: "Then the world will know that you sent me and *have loved them even as you have loved me*" (verse 23, emphasis added). Any one Person of the Trinity is always favoring and deferring to the other two. As Dennis F. Kinlaw reminds us, "If the eternal Son of God protected himself, refused to trust himself to the will of his Father, and ceased to live for someone other than himself, he would cease to be who he is, because God by definition is self-giving love."[26] Jesus suggests that the love of God the Father for you is just like his love for Jesus: "I have made you known to them, and will continue to make you known *in order that the love you have for me may be in them* and that I myself may be in them" (verse 26, emphasis added).

**GLORY.** Glory is God's majestic influence in the universe. It is God's goodness made manifest or on display.[27] I love the word "glory." Jesus prayed, "Father, *I want those you have given me* to be with me where I am, and *to see my glory, the glory you have given me* because you loved me before the creation of the world" (verse 24). In the Hebrew language the root definition of glory is "heavy" or "weighty." The comparable Hebrew word is *kabod* (pronounced "kā-vōd"). A huge stone would, according to this definition, have glory because it is heavy. Sometimes we say "That's a weighty matter." In a sense we are calling the issue glorious.

We learn that when the priest Eli heard that the ark of God had been captured by the Philistines, he fell backward from his chair and broke his neck because he was heavy or glorious (1 Samuel 4:18). Over time weight and heaviness has become a metaphor for "social weight" or influence. Abram, who had lots of cattle, sheep, and servants, was considered to be weighty or glorious—a person of financial influence! "Abram had become very wealthy in livestock and silver and gold," we read in Genesis 13:2. Interestingly, the word here rendered "wealthy" is also *kabod*. When we use the English idiom "throwing one's weight around" we mean that the person wants (to toss into the mix two more idioms) to be a big shot, a mover and a shaker. Now consider our triune God, the God of infinite and majestic influence. The Being in the universe who has the most "weight" is God, and God has every right to throw it around.

THE REAL LORD'S PRAYER

Jesus longs to share his glory with us—to make us co-heirs of that glory. We will be eternally influential.

**JOY.** Joy is mentioned only once in John 17:13: " . . . that they may have the full measure of my joy within them." This is a significant aspect of Jesus' promise to the disciples. Already he had promised that their grief would turn to joy (John 16:20). When the disciples prayed in Jesus' name, God would answer, "so that their joy [would] be complete" (John 16:24). Joy is the inner delightful acknowledgment that the good purposes of God for us are unstoppable. Yes, we continue to suffer struggles of all kinds, but nothing will ever cancel out God's good, loving purposes for us. "For the joy that was set before him he endured the cross," asserts the writer of Hebrews, "scorning its shame, and sat down at the right hand of the throne of God" (Hebrews 12:2). This reality permeates the Trinity forever. C.S. Lewis wrote, "The serious business of heaven in joy." Joy. God, the three-in-one, is eternally delighted in his trinitarian life. And Jesus is anything but stingy with God-joy.

## IMAGINING GOD

I hope that you'll allow me here to indulge in a brief interlude, just to get us back on track. Remember that I urged you not to allow yourself to get bogged down. We are moving in a positive direction, still considering the question "What is your mental image of God?" This issue, as I've pointed out, is crucial for the Christian experience of prayer. As I've encouraged, learn to conceptualize God in terms of "God, the three-in-one." The Trinity. A community of Beings who are in perfect unity—for you, with you, and in you. The oneness, love, glory, and joy that are eternally active in the Trinity together constitute an invitation. Jesus, in effect, prays that we will share in God-unity, God-love, God-glory, and God-joy. Prayer is mysteriously at the same time a one-to-one and a one-to-three conversation. The gift of salvation is an invitation into the circle dance! God, the three-in-one, makes room in the circle for each of us. We are ushered into the relationship that Jesus has eternally enjoyed with his Father. The Spirit *in us* concurs and confirms, motivating us to cry out "*Abba*, Father!"

Now, with the big picture back in focus, I return to what may have seemed a lengthy digression.

**COMMUNICATION.** There is one more fascinating dynamic of trinitarian life for us to explore: communication. The three Persons of the Trinity are engaged in an eternal, loving, unified, joyful, and glorious *conversation*—the primary *perichoretic* dynamic for our praying. John writes in chapter 17:1 of his Gospel, "After Jesus said this, he looked toward heaven and prayed: 'Father, the hour has come . . .'" Jesus the Son, God-in-man, is in continual conversation with God the Father. Graciously, we are invited through Scripture to listen in as God talks to God. Picture Jesus, there in the upper room with his disciples, addressing his Father.

The point I want us to appreciate here is that the trinitarian conversation is eternal and vibrant. In the words of Rebecca Konyndyk DeYoung, "So, in the beginning when there was nothing but God alone, there was communication. From what Jesus says about the inner life of God, apparently one person was speaking to another."[27] God, the three-in-one, is in an eternal conversation with God, the three-in-one. It is into this conversation that we are invited, and it is precisely this inclusion for which our praying heart longs.

About eight years ago I was stunned by the wonder of conversation. So much so that the simple thrill of speech almost left me speechless. Walt and I had met at Panera for some coffee and conversation, and following that meaningful dialogue I walked out of the restaurant in a state of deep-seated amazement. What had just happened? It was a miracle to me. Reflecting on those sacred moments with Walt, I was moved to write this free verse poem:

## The Art of Holy Conversation
John W. Frye

Wrinkles at the corner of the eyes,
a softening inflection of the voice,
a sigh, a slight turn of the head,
a friend speaks to me.
A sacred entity in wearied body
bearing the Image—
priceless, deep imprint of the Other.
Gesturing, fumbling hands,
awkward silences and jump-start
phrases
coming from inside a being,
from a silence unknown to me
except for this series of sounds.
Conversation is a miracle,
a treasure hunt
for meaning, acceptance;
an audio map
Out of the complex wilderness
for two simple, broken wanderers
who drink hot coffee.
Are those wrinkles in the corner of the eyes
or are they branches of the burning bush?
What is this space, other than holy ground?
How is it that our feeble, speaking voices
usher us into the Eternal Silence
where words cannot convey this exact moment?
Holy, holy, holy is this moment almighty!
Two beings, coffee on their breaths,
with puffs of air exchange their souls
on wispy sounds, from very deep to deep!
I walk away from the moment
with a new limp
and
with a new hope,
for I have wrestled with God
in another whom I call
"friend."

If I still today am staggered by my recollection of this simple human conversation, imagine with me what it's like to be invited to participate in the eternal, ongoing dialogue among Father, Son, and Holy Spirit? Like world-class surfers who live to catch the next big wave, we enter breathlessly into the powerful currents of God talking to God—and are invited to join in!

# five

## THE LANGUAGE OF PRAYER

With her consent I include Jill's story "Stick and stones may break my bones, but words will never hurt me." Only later in life do we discover what a despicable lie is carried in that once popular but now debunked children's ditty. Following in her own words is a record of Jill's experience with hurtful words:

> I was invited to a church retreat by a classmate, and since my only exposure to church was when we visited family out of state, I wanted to go. My friend had something I couldn't put my finger on and I wanted it too. It was like a big slumber party that lasted a weekend and I was told how much God loved me personally. On the last day, we were singing hymns and I had never felt anything quite like it. I made so many new friends. The person leading the retreat announced that they had a very special present for us and that by taking this present, we were giving our lives to Christ. Row by row, the kids stood and went up front to get their cross necklaces and take communion. I remember they were given large wooden crosses that were bigger than a pendant on a necklace. I was giddy and full of joy, but when I

got to the end of my row, one of the religious leaders put their arm in front of me and said, "You have to belong to our kind of church to receive a cross and take communion. Go back to your seat." I went back to my seat and was crushed and embarrassed. The rest of the retreat was very dark for me, including the ride home. I didn't tell anyone about it and felt anger at my friend for inviting me. In the words of that religious authority, I felt like God Himself had rejected me. I decided that if that was what God was about, I wanted no part of it. I moved on and stuffed any feelings way down deep. Since God didn't want me I would live life the way I wanted. It wasn't pretty. It wasn't until I started attending church as an adult and had accepted Jesus as my Lord and Savior, that all those feelings came bubbling to the surface. I was told that God loved me right where I was and that everyone was welcome at the table. That was life-changing and in the years since, God has provided crosses/communion in many forms, covering me in love and grace. Just over a year ago, I was asked to lead a women's retreat, and I chose the theme of the weekend to be "It's All About Jesus." The song I chose was "Amazing Love" and the verse I chose was Philippians 4:13, I can do all things through Christ who strengthens me. God has brought healing to all of my sin and shame.

I was there the day Jill was baptized. I listened to her story, stunned to think of a young girl so happy to learn about Jesus and God's love, so eager to receive the gifts of a cross and take communion, so devastated that in the voice of one of God's servants she heard "God doesn't want you." To this day Jill's story causes me to shudder.

"The tongue has the power of life and death and those who love it will eat its fruit," says Proverbs 18:21. When I preached and taught about Jesus, the good shepherd of John 10, people would regularly let me know how much Jesus' words about the shepherd meant to them: "He calls his own sheep by name and leads them out. . . . I am the good shepherd; I know my sheep and my sheep know me" (John 10:3, 14). Folks were thrilled, marveling, "God knows me *by name*. I am not just a face lost in the crowds of billions of people!" There is life in Jesus' words.

I personally never experienced that kind of exhilaration based on those verses. Only later in life did I find out why. My father, who walked out of my life because of divorce when I was ten years old, had never called me by my name. He had called me "boy," as in "What's the boy doing?" or "Where's the boy?" or "Get in here, boy!" My mother shared this with me when I was around forty-two years old. Searching my memory, I realized with a start that this was true.

At one point as I was pouring out my soul about my troubled childhood to a seasoned pastor and wise counselor, he addressed this issue as follows: "John, you need to grieve this. It's not right that a father would never address his son by name. It's not what God intended, nor did God ever intend for a father to abandon his own son."

I remember sitting in a living room chair shortly thereafter in the middle of the night. In the darkened silence I acknowledged my longing to be addressed by my dad as "John." The tears came. And in the honesty of the tears, healing followed. What was done was done. My dad had died at the age of sixty-four. Now, as I poured out my wounds to God, the part of me that had atrophied based on his unfortunate word choices was resurrected and restored in the life and love of my heavenly Father. Human speech is powerful—for good or ill—in shaping the souls of people.

The concept of communication in prayer brings up the seemingly straightforward issue of speech, as in our ability to talk to one another. Have you ever paused and reflected on the miracle of speech? The very idea that we can transmit ideas, dreams, hurts, and information from one person to another through mere puffs of wind that carry sounds can be startling beyond comprehension. Imagine that you and I are sitting at coffee talking about prayer. Puffs of wind from our mouths are conveying epic truths for our lives. A miracle, indeed. So much life!

*Speech begins with God.* Our God is a speaking God, and his speaking results in creation. Words, after all, brought the universe into existence. Resounding through Genesis 1 is the recurring phrase "And God said . . . !" Idols have mouths but cannot speak . . . unless we're talking about a surround-sound TV.

In creation God makes human beings in his own image and likeness. A vital aspect of God's image in us is our godlike capacity to speak. Leonard Verduin writes, "Because [a human being] is a creature of speech, his relationship with his Maker is likewise *speech-related*, so that the very idea of personal relationship between the two is *dependent upon communication* between them"[28] (emphasis added).

Our capability to produce and understand speech opens the door to a tremendous relationship that is embedded in prayer. Verduin writes concerning this relationship, "The prayer that is not a *response* is not prayer in the right key note. The only prayer acceptable in the ears of the Communicator is embroidery on the Communicator's communication. Prayers, too, must be in the form of playback; if prayer is not in the idiom of the Word it is in a false idiom."[29] Verduin echoes Eugene Peterson's point that prayer is answering speech.

As we consider the miracle of our ability to communicate, to speak, to "say the word" (or, as in our present context, "to speak the Word"), we begin to sense an emergence in our thinking. We begin to grasp the important role of Scripture in the structuring of our prayer life. Indeed, the wonder of God's words to human beings has been codified. That simply means that God's Word, powerful and creative as it is, has been written down for all to hear and read. This truth is absolute miracle. When we hold our Bible we are holding a supernatural wonder!

## OUR WORDY WORLD

Prayer words, like any others, can become numerous and empty. Henri J. M. Nouwen has this to say on the subject:

> Recently I was driving through Los Angeles, and suddenly I had the strange sensation of driving through a huge dictionary. Wherever I looked there were words trying to take my eyes off the road. They said, "Use me, take me, buy me, drink me, smell

me, touch me, kiss me, sleep with me." In such a world who can maintain respect for words? All this is to suggest that words; my own included, have lost their creative power. Their limitless multiplication has made us lose confidence in words, and caused us to think, more often than not, "They are just words."[30]

I have spoken with many couples over the years who were experiencing marital difficulty. Most often a core breakdown in their relationship had to do with lack of and/or faulty communication. "He just won't talk to me," the wife declares. "She is always telling me what a failure I am. I can't do anything right," the husband laments. Speech has become a weapon: "The poison of asps is under their lips," as the King James Version so graphically renders Romans 3:13. A husband will say to me, "I tell her all the time that I love her." The wife looks glaringly at him: "Yeah, but it's just words. *You're* just words. Show me you love me." Just words. Someone has said that communication constitutes the nervous system of a marriage. You stop talking and you have injured the spinal cord of love. A husband and wife become paralyzed as marriage partners.

Prayer words must transcend "just words." Of all the ways in which words are cheapened in our culture, we may not let the language of prayer degenerate into flimsy disposability. God has given us a tremendous gift that keeps the words of our praying heart robust, significant, and creative. God through his living Word has given us sacred words—yes, prayer words—perhaps most notably in the magnificent book of Psalms (as well as in other prayers recorded in the Bible, as, for example, Jesus' prayer in John 17 and Paul's in Ephesians 3:14–21).

## THE LANGUAGE MAP

I am indebted to Eugene H. Peterson for the following overview of three types of language. Peterson, who noted that a writer needs to be "a shepherd of words,"[31] instilled in me a fascination for the way language works. The "language map" is found in his book *Answering God: The Psalms as Tools for Prayer.*[32] I have taken some liberty in adapting these language types for this section of the book.

Language I—to create relationships: relational language

Language II—to name things: informational language

Language III—to make things happen: motivational language

## LANGUAGE III

Let's work backward, starting with Language III. This language, in the words of Larry the Cable guy, is "Git 'er done!" It makes things happen and motivates people to move or decide. It is the language of politics:

"Vote for me!"

"Contribute today!"

And it's the word of advertising:

"Buy it and be happy!"

"On sale. Get it now!"

"But wait! There's more . . . !"

In a consumer society like the United States, this use of words is designed to extract money from our wallet and transfer it into the hands of product-producers. The force of Language III is imperatives, commands: "Don't run into the street!" "At-TEN-tion!" "At ease." This language seeks to move people. The overall purpose is "getting things done."

The dark side of Language III is that it can become manipulative. You have received those friendly "courtesy calls" in which the caller wants to get you to say "yes" just once, to just one question. When you do, you're sucked into a complicated marketing ploy to get you signed up for the deal of a lifetime.

Sadly, certain forms of personal evangelism have bought in to the "marketing model" of salvation. The vacuum cleaner salesperson asks, "In view of this top-of-the-line vacuum and how it just cleaned the mess from your carpet and its amazing low, low price, is there any reason you can think of that would keep you from buying it?" And some evangelism approaches ask, "In light of God's love for you by having Jesus die on the cross for your sins, is there any reason you shouldn't pray and receive him into your life right now so you can go to heaven when you die?" Jesus isn't a product, and neither is the salvation God offers.

## LANGUAGE II

Language II is informational language. It names and defines things, including concepts. Door. Wall. Tree. Hand. Water. Gravity. Capitalism. Injustice. Astronomy. It provides labels to help us navigate our world. We are able to orient ourselves in a specific space. The force of this language is declarative. It is the language of education, of knowledge. Certain disciplines use special words. The language of medicine is different from that of law. The language of theology is different from that of sports. The overall purpose of this language is "knowing."

This "knowing" language can be sneaky and even insidious, moving in and pretending to be the language of prayer. Talking about stuff can substitute for vital conversation in marriage. Men tend to be masters at communicating the "facts" about their day. Many wives could care less about the facts; they want to know how their husbands feel about life—in particular, about their life together. Wives have said to me, "I don't care how many widgets he made at work today. I want to know if he still likes his job. Is he happy, fulfilled? Does he hate it?" We can convey factual truth and at the same time be telling emotional lies. What's in your heart—not just in your head? Did you know that the devil is the father of lies? The devil doesn't care if you believe a factual lie (the earth is flat) or an emotional lie (God doesn't love me as much as he loves other people). The devil will take whatever lie you believe and seek to destroy you with it.

The apostle Paul wrote, "Knowledge puffs up, but love builds up" (1 Corinthians 8:1). Knowledge can become competitive. That happened among the Christians in Corinth. Some Corinthian believers felt superior based on what they "knew" in comparison to the knowledge base of others. They were "puffed up," as though they were an A+, elite class of Christian. Knowledge can separate. Create divisions. Fracture community.

Academic knowledge can become very elitist. We look for the best-trained, most knowledgeable doctors, lawyers, mechanics, and plumbers. We sport "Proud Parents of an Honor Student" bumper stickers.

Paul preferred love. Love will not compete in any way other than to stoop the lowest and to serve at its best. New Testament scholar Craig L. Bloomberg had this to say about 1 Corinthians 8:1: "Love rather than knowledge remains the center of Paul's ethics (cf. Galatians 5:14) and the highest form of human virtues, without which all spiritual gifts prove worthless (1 Corinthians 13). This kind of love is sacrificial self-giving, centered around and imitating Christ's cross-work, not primarily a nice feeling, familial friendship, or mere altruism."[33] Love truly shines in Language I:

## LANGUAGE I

Language I is relational language, and its purpose is to create and promote relationships. This is the language of lovers, poets, and pray-ers. It's the language of parents to their infant children: "Say 'Mama.'" "Say 'Papa.'" "Say 'pasta'"—which in my mind certainly means "Say 'Grandpa.'" Cry "*Abba*, Father."

This is what Peterson calls "first language." Its force is *being*—being in relationship. Imagine a mother leaning over the crib listening to the coos and gurgles of her baby. The mother says, "My little booboo. I just wubwubwub oo. Boo bada baa boo." The baby gurgles back nonsense sounds. What is happening here? Nonsense . . . or an indescribably profound verbal exchange? With nonsense sounds and infantile words a relationship of love, trust, and hope is being established. No content is communicated and no command uttered. Yet love bonds two human beings! Love creates communion and community.

Consider the whisper of "sweet nothings" in a lover's ear. At least while men are dating, they tend to be adept at language I. They write poems to their beloved. I don't know why, but it seems as though this ability shuts down completely when he hears his woman utter "I do" on their wedding day. She may gradually come to hear not sweet nothings but virtually *nothing*. This is a lament I have heard too often in my years as a pastor.

Language I doesn't try to know or sell anything. It doesn't intend to educate or motivate. It's simply the language of being. Of being together. And *Language I is the language of prayer.*

Of course, as we read the psalms, other Bible prayers, and other formulaic or pre-composed (written) prayers, we will come across a treasure of good information. We will even be exposed to some sharp commands: "Wake up, God! Why are you not paying attention to me?!" Yet, overall, prayer language is first or original language. It's all about that "personal relationship with God" the gospel claims to establish for us. Your heart, filled with and prompted by the Spirit, does indeed cry "*Abba*, Father."

Language I does not exclude Languages II and III. We have to recognize that those two languages together constitute the dominant, often verbose clamor of our culture. We are bombarded with facts we need to know, tantalized with things we need to buy, and guilt-tripped about acts we need to do. In the midst of this in-our-faces pressure, we seek to express the language of the soul. The relationship-building speech of the praying heart. This is where the psalms come in.

I listened to a talk by Richard Rohr, a Franciscan friar, on a CD. In his conclusion he led the listeners in a brief prayer based on Psalm 46:10: "Be still and know that I am God." Rohr stressed the importance of just "being" in the presence of God. Not doing, not praying, not trying to figure things out. Rohr invited his listeners to

"Repeat after me . . .
"Be still and know that I am God." (repeat)
"Be still and know that I AM." (repeat)
"Be still and know." (repeat)
"Be still." (repeat)
"Be." (repeat)

Rohr went silent. He had led the listeners into God's presence, inviting us in the end to be silent and, more profoundly, to *be*. I have used this prayer with my congregation many times. In a world of hurry—think trying to get yourself and your family to church on time—this is a settling, centering prayer with which to begin a worship service.

## THE PSALMS

The psalms are the school of prayer. No one has said this more clearly and simply than Eugene H. Peterson in his book *Answering God: The Psalms as Tools for Prayer*. Let's recall that praying, in essence, is answering God. God and his communication are first; our words in prayer are forever a response. "The Psalms are acts of obedience," declares Peterson, "answering the God who addresses us. God's word precedes these words: These prayers don't seek God, they respond to the God who seeks us."[34]

Your praying heart was created for the psalms as much as your breathing lungs were created for oxygen. Yet, while growing up in churches, many of us were never told this. We learned a model of personal, spontaneous prayer. Written, formulaic prayers, including those from a prayer book, were considered less than real or authentic and therefore suspect. We learned that "real prayers" are formulated on the spot and usually concern immediate issues at hand. Even mouthing "the Lord's Prayer," so the thinking goes, can degenerate into nothing more than "vain repetition."

There is nothing wrong with personal, spontaneous prayers. Yet if they constitute the sum total of our prayer life, we will gradually lose our motivation to pray. Beyond that, our own spontaneous prayers will invariably begin to sound more and more like vain repetitions in that we all tend to repeat the same elements—even if we move beyond petition to include praise, intercession, and repentance—over and over again. "Thank you, God, for food and family." I have often been embarrassed by my own mealtime prayers. Talk about pathetic, empty repetition. *Am I really saying this stuff again? Is there no originality or growth in me?* I wouldn't have been surprised had I opened my eyes after a mealtime prayer to see my wife and four daughters asleep in their plates of spaghetti.

How ironic that we can begin to practice the very thing we were warned to avoid. To save us from hollow, repetitive words in prayer, God has provided an arsenal of prayer-words titled the Book of Psalms. Almost every prayer master I have read at some point sets before his readers the book of Psalms, saying in effect, "Here they are. These are the words for which your praying heart yearns. Here, through these prayers, you are invited to join God talking to God through human beings."

The Trappist monk Andrè Louf offers an astounding truth about the psalms. Read carefully his wise observations:

> In their naked and literal aspect the psalms are at once poetry and prayer: prayer, indeed, but in poetic form. Their potency, however, is *not merely a human thing. God is Himself using and producing the word* that they address to [humanity]. That word is instinct, not only with the living breath of a human individual— albeit that of a creator-poet—but also with the breath of God, who is creator-Spirit. . . . [T]he psalms have a special place. In the Scriptures God utters His Word to man. With the psalms it is just the other way round. *Here God puts into the mouth of man the Word that man is to offer Him in response*[35] (emphasis added).

Louf is saying that the Creator-Spirit has given his words to us through the creator-poets (the psalmists) so that when we pray human words we are in fact coming full circle to pray back the very words of God. Think about that!

This is hardly news to those who believe that our Bibles are filled with books breathed out (inspired) by God.

> *All Scripture is God-breathed* and is useful for teaching, rebuking, correcting and training in righteousness. (2 Timothy 3:16, emphasis added)

Even though we know that God used human agents like Moses, David, Isaiah, Mark, Luke, Paul, John, and many others to create them, we refer to the Bible as *God's Word*. The Bible is, indeed, both God's Word and human words (God's Word expressed through Spirit-inspired human words, phraseology, and style). Indeed, the psalms are prayers inspired by God the Spirit, who supervised the human poets who prayed and penned them. When you pray the psalms you are praying God-prayers. And these divine prayers set your praying heart aflame!

Think of the psalms as an invitation into the conversation of God talking to God. God the Spirit inspired the words of the psalms, and the human poets—David, Moses, the sons of Korah, and others—were God's agents to write these songs. The psalms together constitute both a prayer book and a hymnbook. As you pray them the Spirit sends these words back to God through the conduit of your praying heart. You join with God, talking to God with God-words. You are joining the *perichoretic* conversation! Is it any wonder that the most quoted book by Jesus and by the New Testament writers is the book of Psalms?

Scot McKnight, a good friend and distinguished New Testament and Jesus scholar (not to mention a Chicago Cubs fan), writes,

> Jesus was a master of the psalms. Wherever he heard them, in the synagogue and at the temple, he took them to heart, for the psalms spilled constantly from his lips. Because of this, anyone who follows Jesus into the Church to pray will quickly learn that praying with Jesus means using the psalms. His entire life was bathed with psalms. . . . The book of Psalms was the first teacher and the mentor in prayer for all of Judaism.[36]

N. T. Wright, a New Testament scholar and a historian of Jesus and of the early church, has written a book titled *The Case for the Psalms: Why They are Essential.* Wright, too, observes:

> As you sing the Psalms, pray the Psalms, and ponder the Psalms, you will find yourself drawn into a world in which certain things make sense that would not otherwise do so. In particular, you will be drawn *into a world where God and Jesus make sense in a way they would not otherwise do. . . .* The Psalms are the steady, sustained subcurrent of healthy Christian living.

*They shaped the praying and vocation of Jesus.* They can and will do the same for us[37] (emphasis added).

In the same way God created air for your breathing lungs, *he created the psalms for your praying heart.* The psalms offer a new vocabulary for the new heart God gave you as a fascinating reality of the new covenant. Your new heart will soar into the presence of God as you pray the psalms. When you turn and look back into your life, into your relationships, and into the world, you will see it all with new eyes. The eyes of your heart will have been enlightened. In Paul's words, "I pray that the eyes of your heart may be enlightened in order that you may know the hope to which he has called you, the riches of his glorious inheritance in his holy people" (Ephesians 1:18).

## PSALMS AND THE CHURCH

Are the psalms really that prominent in the life of the church? We have already learned about Jesus and the book of Psalms. But what about ordinary Christians like ourselves? Let's take a closer look at two verses from the apostle Paul:

> Do not get drunk on wine, which leads to debauchery. Instead, be filled with the Spirit, *speaking to one another with psalms,* hymns, and songs from the Spirit. Sing and make music from your heart to the Lord, always giving thanks to God the Father for everything, in the name of our Lord Jesus Christ. (Ephesians 5:18–20, emphasis added)

Do you notice the reference to psalms? I can't help but wonder which psalms Paul had in mind. Could it be that the early church, in its Spirit-filled worship, truly did speak to God and to one another through the language of the psalms? Some of these believers would have been converted Gentiles who had no prior knowledge of the rich scriptural treasure God had given to—and to the Gentile converts through—the Jewish people. Yet these believers were here enjoined by Paul to speak to one another "with psalms." How important that compilation of hymnody must have been to the apostle

Paul and the new churches. Paul reiterates the theme in addressing another church:

> Let the peace of Christ rule in your hearts, since as members of one body you were called to peace. And be thankful. Let the message of Christ dwell among you richly as you teach and *admonish one another with all wisdom through psalms*, hymns, and songs from the Spirit, singing to God with gratitude in your hearts. And whatever you do, whether in word or deed, do it all in the name of the Lord Jesus, giving thanks to God the Father through him. (Colossians 3:15–17, emphasis added)

Again in the gathering of the church in Colossae for fellowship and worship, the book of Psalms comes into prominent focus. Picture Gentiles who have converted to the Messiah of the Jews—to the Lord of the universe—admonishing one another with "all wisdom" through the language of the psalms. In the life of Christ and his Church the psalms find a prominent place in speech, prayer, and worship. Who of us hasn't called out to the Lord for wisdom? I wonder whether God our Father might not sigh a little before commenting to the Son and the Spirit, "You know, I already gave them wisdom . . . in the psalms."

The psalms, then, are useful for more than private prayer. This compilation may be claimed and utilized as the prayer book of today's church, just as it was in Ephesus and Colossae. Scot McKnight refers to private prayer as "praying *in* the church" and to communal prayer as "praying *with* the church."[38] Both are vital for our growth.

## ALL OF LIFE MATTERS

The psalms show us that every human emotion is legitimate, even our anger and hatred. The psalms invite us into whole prayer. These God-inspired songs present the full range of human experience, from the highest ecstasy to the deepest despair and everything in between. The psalms variously depict the poets as happy; spitefully angry; and enraged at God, at others, and at themselves. The psalmists don't hesitate to bring it all and to lay it all before

God. The psalms invite us to be totally, fully human in the presence of God.

You might find yourself experiencing a pleasant time; your life for the time being is good. You read a psalm or two and are blasted with anger or despair, for cries for help and deliverance. You might conclude "This just isn't speaking to me today." But is that really the point? What if—just what if—you are praying those psalms on behalf of those countless thousands in the world who *are* currently hurt, defeated, oppressed, or seemingly without hope? You have become a global intercessor in your faithful reading and praying of the psalms.

On the other hand, you might find yourself in a state of despondency, anxiety, confusion, or anger yet read two happy psalms, overflowing with exuberant praise for blessings. "This is just not where I am today," you might say to yourself. But as you read the seemingly out-of-sync-with-your-life words, a strange and unexpectedly solid hope emerges in your soul: the Spirit whispers, almost audibly, "It won't always be this way. There may be tears at night, but joy will come in the morning."

The safest place to take our sometimes miserable humanity and our sometimes majestic life is into the presence of God. The psalms invite us to do just that, and they provide us with laser-sharp vocabulary with which to articulate our response.

## PSALMS AND THE "DARK NIGHT"

I served a church for twenty-four years as teaching pastor. The church was a vibrant, "cutting edge" community of believers, creative risk-takers who were committed to loving God and loving people. During the last two of those twenty-four years, however, the ugly head of conflict reared up in ways I had never before experienced. The leaders were divided, and the congregation became factious on an epic scale. Peacemaker that I am, I tried hard to get the folks to voice their concerns and reconcile. It didn't happen. The horses were out of the barn and couldn't be corralled. All of this turmoil plunged me into the darkest night of my soul. Glimpsing no glimmer of light at the end of the long, dark tunnel, I became depleted, questioning God on every turn—even physically ill from not eating or sleeping. I was what is medically called "a basket case"—an emotional wreck, engulfed in agonizing anxiety and dark despair. During this time I still had to prepare messages and preach. I hated it.

The psalms. I read the psalms. Not the happy ones. No, I gravitated to the dark, despairing ones. Think Psalm 88:5: "I am set apart with the dead, like the slain who lie in the grave, whom you remember no more, who are cut off from your care." These inspired-by-God words kept me sane, I do confess. No, reading them didn't make me "feel good." But the exercise did give me a "by the skin of my teeth" hope that it was okay to be in that place and that it was not always going to be that way. As I have since shared with others, "I held on to those psalms by my fingernails. I no longer had a firm grasp on God, on myself, or on ministry."

Beyond my own limited wisdom, conflicted feelings, and seemingly out-of-control circumstances, God's Word resident in these psalms of despair became my words. Mysteriously, yet tangibly, they kept me alive and persistently expectant for some kind of turnaround in my life.

The turnaround came. As hard as that "dark night" had been, in retrospect I wouldn't have changed a thing. The lessons I learned about God, about myself, about ministry in the local church, and about life I could not have gleaned in any other way. The cliché rang true for me: no pain, no gain. As my counselor informed me, "Depression is God's way of slamming us into reality." I learned to relate to God in his apparent absence, despite having no sense whatsoever of his loving, powerful, purposeful presence (a hard lesson, for sure). I learned to de-idolize my views of church and ministry, and I discovered that I was more broken than I could ever have imagined. How deeply I resonated with the poignant words of Psalm 51:17: "My sacrifice, O God, is a broken spirit; a broken and contrite heart, you, God, will not despise."

Before I offer you some guidance on the use of the psalms in your own prayer life, it's imperative that we explore one crucial reality. We must take seriously the marble slab engulfing our vulnerable, pulsating heart. You are a praying person, and you have a praying heart. The process of liberation necessitates jack-hammering away the solid stone encasing our hearts. Our praying heart's voice will then be heard—not only by God but, yes, *by us*. Our liberated heart will begin to shape our ongoing prayer life.

We need this to enable us to joyfully and intentionally engage with God, the three-in-one, in the great eternal, loving conversation. We'll go on from here to examine the resistant layers of granite blocking you from hearing the whispers and whimpers of your own praying heart. Let me repeat: just because you are a praying person in possession of an ever-praying heart does not mean you have nothing to do to experience a renewed prayer life. The process will include this wonderful truth from the apostle Paul: "Therefore, my dear friends, as you have always obeyed—not only in my presence, but now much more in my absence—*continue to work out your salvation* with fear and trembling, for it is God who works in you to will and to act in order to fulfill his good purpose" (Philippians 2:12–13, emphasis added). We work out what God has worked in. This is a liberation process, not just a learning process.

# six

## CARVING AWAY THE STONE

Michelangelo is reported to have had a photographic memory. He would sketch his figure, select his block of marble, and then make precise miniature models out of wax or terra cotta. Finally, he would set about carving the large block of marble, using the small models as his guide. Interestingly, he usually carved the torso first if the statue was of a human being.[39] I find it fascinating that he started with that portion of the body that contained the heart.

There are layers of granite blocking your praying heart, and in order to free it you'll have to recognize, discern, and chip away at the stone. Like Michelangelo, start small. Don't try to liberate your praying heart too quickly. This process isn't microwavable; it isn't a 100-meter dash. It takes patience. This is art—soul art. Take your time.

### THE LAYERS OF GRANITE

Because so many people desire to pray well and because each person is unique, there must be millions of variations of stone layers that block the praying heart. I will describe three of the most prominent obstacles in the hope that whatever is blocking your praying heart will be a variation of one of these. The three are:

Layer 1: "I've tried and failed." This is the layer of disappointment because of unanswered prayer.
Layer 2: "God knows everything already. Why pray?" This is the layer of faulty teaching and thinking about prayer.
Layer 3: "I just know I *ought to* learn to pray." This is the layer of religious obligation that carries with it both pressure and guilt.

## LAYER 1

Let's consider each layer individually. Layer 1 is driven by "my experience." I have tried to pray and God just doesn't hear—or worse—doesn't care. Scot McKnight writes about this layer honestly, clearly, and fully:

The single biggest discouragement in prayer is unanswered, deeply felt petitions. . . . I have no answer to the problem of unanswered prayer, and frankly the typical answers don't do much for me—that God does answer but not in the way we expected, that we are to keep on praying, that we are out of God's will, that our motives are impure, that we are really only learning to adjust our will to God's will, that we really don't want what we are asking, that the answers are given as "yes, no, or wait a little longer." None of these really get to the heart of the heartfelt yearning for God to act. I don't appeal to mystery. Instead, I focus on who God is, and I continue to lay my petitions before God in faith, trust, and hope. Sometimes hope lags behind our petitions, and sometimes hope sustains us. But I keep on praying because I believe God is good. Sometimes it is discouraging, and I'd be a liar if I didn't admit it.[40]

Let's probe to the soul of this layer. Why do we pray? Only to get answers? If that's the case, if we don't get them are we justified in concluding that God's doesn't hear or care? I do believe that God cares about how we feel, but I think it is dangerous to conclude anything about his character based on our own experience of unanswered prayer. It's a great leap from my discouragement over unanswered prayer to a detrimental view of the character of God—not to mention that this is a dangerous leap for the soul.

If I could summarize Scot McKnight's confession, I'd say "Unanswered prayer sucks." But I would avoid even the suggestion of a conclusion that God's character is in any way deficient. Scot continues to pray, not because he holds out a glimmer of hope of getting a "belated" answer but because God is good. What Dr. McKnight doesn't try to do is find comfort in some great "mystery" of God in an attempt to ease the pain of unanswered prayer. In and despite the pain and discouragement, he would certainly advocate, the believer continues to pray. So many life issues taken to God go unanswered: not being able to conceive a child, find a marriage partner, or reconcile with an alienated spouse, for example, or not getting that healing from cancer you so passionately desire. I don't know what your unanswered prayer issues are. I only ask that you not let them develop into a hard rock obstacle to your praying heart.

A great church Mother, Julian of Norwich, wrote, "God only desires that our soul cling to him with all its strength, in particular, that it clings to his goodness. For of all of the things our minds can think about God, it is thinking upon his goodness that pleases him most and brings the most profit to our soul."[41]

So many times I have read that although life doesn't always seem good God is always good. That invariably comes as a timely reminder. Nor is the church always good. The very people who are called to represent God in the world too often fail to do so. *Represent.* Look at the word, and break it down into its components: re-present. If only the church would re-present to the world the true God, revealed in Jesus of Nazareth! How many young people would decline to walk away from the church and from God if the church were to authentically represent God as revealed in Jesus.

It isn't healthy to blame a bad life on a good God. This thought leads me to the next solid layer of granite constricting our praying hearts.

## LAYER 2

Layer 2 is so hard because it is depends on a faulty view of God's will and the place of prayer in it. "Since God already knows what will happen (or, if you're a Calvinist, "God knows what will happen because *God decreed* it to happen that way"), then why pray?" Prayer makes no difference. *Que sera sera*—"whatever will be, will be." Why bother asking God for anything because God already knows and/or has planned the future.

I remember a meeting in Bible college when one of the professors conducted a voluntary session with students about the sovereignty of God. The session was not in the academic schedule; the teacher wanted to speak personally. We met after class hours in a lecture hall. The teacher bluntly offered a view of the sovereignty of God that obliterated the whole point of prayer. The session caused quite a stir among the students. It so happened that not long afterward that professor was released from the faculty.

It was during those days that I learned a lot about God's sovereignty and human free will. Yes, the students debated informally, and sometimes vehemently, in the coffee shops and hallways and on campus grounds. But campus debates among students can be safe and academic. Not so in the real world of the local church.

## GOD HELD HER UNDER

This is a true story, and I have changed the names. Years ago Joe asked to meet with me at a local restaurant. His wife, Cathy, had a brain tumor that was thought to be terminal. Thankfully, Cathy made it through the medical crisis and became once again healthy and active. (By the way, I saw both Joe and Cathy about three weeks ago at the supermarket.)

In our one on one meeting at the restaurant, Joe expressed happiness on one level because his wife had survived, but he was very angry

LIBERATE YOUR PRAYING HEART

at God on a deeper level, challenging me, "John, imagine God taking my wife out into Lake Michigan in about neck-high water. This strong God pushes her under until she begins to flail. She comes up gasping for air, and God forces her under again. This keeps happening, and our family and I have to watch helplessly from the shore. Suddenly God releases Cathy and she walks back to shore—alive, yes, but having been forced to endure a horrible ordeal. Am I really supposed to praise God and say 'Thank you, thank you, thank you, God'? God held her under and God let her go. So for this I am supposed to praise him? I can't do it."

A prevailing stronghold against prayer is the view that everything is planned by—or, in a softer-sounding version, allowed by God; it really makes no difference. Somehow God is in *total control* of all things. In theology this view is driven by God's eternal, all-inclusive (even the movements of nano-particles are planned by God), immutable (unchanging) decree (plan). If you think about this view long enough, you will go bonkers. In this scenario there is indeed a deadly layer of impenetrable stone restricting the praying heart.

## GOD GUIDED THE BULLET?

Some missionaries from our part of Michigan experienced a tragic event in South America. Their missionary plane, presumed by authorities to be running drugs, was shot at, and the missionary's wife and child were both killed by a single bullet. An article in our local newspaper reported the missionary as saying, in effect, that God guided the bullet that killed his wife and child.[42] While I can't imagine the pain in this man's life caused by such a tragic event, I was troubled by his comment because of the image of God it offered. *What?!* I wanted to shout. *No! Don't paint this vision of God before the newspaper readers of our city!* This is such deficient teaching. Such destructive theology.

I appeal once again to my pastor-scholar friend Scot McKnight, who writes, "I believe that the broad sweep of the way in which prayer works in the Bible—and I'm thinking here of Jonah and repentance of the Ninevites—teaches us that God in his

**67**

sovereignty has established a kind of contingency in the universe, and that God *genuinely interacts* with humans who pray in such a way that the universe changes as a result of our prayer."[43]

If we believe in some meticulous, inviolable plan of God that causes all events to take place, we are left with a God who becomes at times a monster. God is an intensely relational being, with Father, Son, and Spirit continuously interacting in unity, love, glory, and joy. God created us in his own image, so that we, too, are relational beings. Prayer is a deeply relational, conversational reality. Scot stresses that the Bible presents a view of prayer in which God genuinely interacts with people and realities in the universe actually change based on prayer. Scot mentions Jonah and the people of Nineveh:

> "Then the word of the Lord came to Jonah a second time: 'Go to the great city of Nineveh and proclaim to it the message I give you.' Jonah obeyed the word of the Lord and went to Nineveh. Now Nineveh was a very large city; it took three days to go through it. Jonah began by going a day's journey into the city, proclaiming, 'Forty more days and Nineveh will be overthrown.' The Ninevites believed God. A fast was proclaimed, and all of them, from the greatest to the least, put on sackcloth."
> *(Jonah 3:1–5)*

Nineveh, the capital of the Assyrian empire, was home to a violent, oppressive people, who had destroyed Samaria and taken captive the northern kingdom of Israel in 722 b.c. Jonah had every reason to hate the Ninevites, and we can on the human level understand his desire to flee from God and God's mission for him. Jonah understood that the God of Israel and Judah was good, patient, and forgiving.

When Jonah finally got to Nineveh and followed through with his assignment of preaching imminent judgment, the whole city, from the king down, repented in sackcloth and ashes: "When God saw what they did," we read, "and how they turned from their evil ways, he relented and did not bring on them the destruction he had threatened" (Jonah 3:10).

God *relented*. A similar word, used only of humans, is "repented." God had charged his prophet Jonah to proclaim judgment . . . in just forty days. The people heard the message, took it to heart, and turned from their sin. And God, in direct response, also turned: in keeping with his faithful character, he did an about face, moving from his judgment mode to his mercy mode. "This does not diminish him [God]," points out Andrè Louf. "Far from it. He would be a lesser God if he could not change his intentions when he thinks it is appropriate."[44] Ours is a relational God—a God who genuinely interacts with his people and responds to contingencies in the universe based on their behavior, repentance, and intercession..

Let's consider one more biblical example: King Hezekiah's story, as told in Isaiah 38. This episode is highly instructive about God's interaction with his people when they pray. I offer for your consideration verses 1–6:

> In those days Hezekiah became ill and was at the point of death. The prophet Isaiah son of Amoz went to him and said, "This is what the LORD says: put your house in order, because you are going to die; you will not recover."
>
> Hezekiah turned his face to the wall and prayed to the LORD, "Remember, LORD, how I have walked before you faithfully and with wholehearted devotion and have done what is good in your eyes." And Hezekiah wept bitterly.
>
> Then the word of the LORD came to Isaiah: "Go and tell Hezekiah, 'This is what the LORD, the God of your father David, says: I have heard your prayer and seen your tears; I will add fifteen years to your life. And I will deliver you and this city from the hand of the king of Assyria. I will defend this city.'"

We are seeing firsthand the relationship God has with one of his prophets, Isaiah, and with one of his kings, Hezekiah. The Babylonians are threatening to storm Jerusalem and to destroy the temple and city. Hezekiah, in a move to appease the Babylonians, shows them all the gold of the temple service implements. For this he is stricken with an illness, which God reports, through Isaiah, to be the result of his judgment. God says to Isaiah, "Go tell Hezekiah, 'The LORD says . . .'" Now when God says he is going to do something, we can bank on its being done. The old King James Version renders this emphatic terminology as "Thus saith the LORD!" The prophetic word was "You are going to die, King Hezekiah. You will not recover. This saith the LORD."

Hezekiah, heart-stricken, prayed with bitter tears that God would heal him. But wait. The decree. "Thus saith the LORD" had to stand. Or did it?

Something amazing happens instead. Imagine Isaiah resting in his room somewhere in the palace complex when the Lord speaks to him: "Go tell the king he is not going to die." A bewildered Isaiah asks, "How can this be? I went to the king with a 'Thus saith the LORD' on my lips. What kind of wishy-washy prophet do you think I am? If I go in there now with *this* word, I'll lose all credibility! Not to mention, LORD, that your holy, unchanging word is on the line!"

But God insists, "Isaiah, go and say to Hezekiah, 'The LORD says, "I will add 15 years to your life.'" Once again we read it ("Thus saith the LORD")—followed by a proclamation quite opposite God's initial pronouncement. In essence, we see here the juxtaposition of two divine decrees: "Thus saith the LORD, 'you will die'" and "Thus saith the LORD, you will not die.'" A loving, relational, compassionate, forgiving God heard and genuinely interacted in mercy with King Hezekiah.

Don't allow a faulty view of God's sovereignty to put its squeeze around your heart. Instead, rejoice that God is all-powerful, that his purposes are secure, and that he loves and longs to interact with you. I've always thought a line of logic beginning like this to be ironic: if we accept Jesus we'll enter into a "personal relationship with God." So far, so good, right? But later on we encounter some deep theology, and God becomes in our mind the most impersonal, controlling, unchanging, unfeeling Being imaginable. Dallas Willard describes this presentation of God as "a great unblinking cosmic Stare."[45] Read through your Bible, letting *it*—not some stagnant version of systematic theology—set the framework for your praying heart.

## LAYER 3

The third layer of granite consists of a formidable obstacle to prayer that carries the force of years of religious conditioning. This is the sense of a binding Christian obligation: "We just have to, ought to, need to *learn* to pray."

Before we consider the third layer let's take a breather. The endeavor to free your praying heart is a process—just as sculpting a marble statue is a process. As you chisel away the rock that constricts your praying heart, you will sense a stirring. Faint cries will seem to become more noticeable. Proceed slowly here, yet with great anticipation. Another wonderful church Mother, Catherine of Genoa, wrote, "When God gives light to the soul, it no longer desires to live with that part of it that continues to block the light."[46] Substitute for "light" the emerging voice of your praying heart. Then let the blocks fall and move on.

Layer 3 is the religiously based obstacle. Since I became a believer (as a junior high teen), I have been handed over the years a boatload of exhortations to pray. You *must* pray, I was repeatedly told. My soul was overloaded with ought to's, need to's, have to's, and shoulds—most from well-intentioned, goodhearted people who wanted me to progress in my Christian growth. But the sense of *obligation* served only to cancel out the compelling *invitation* of the God who had implanted within me my praying heart. An invitation is courteous and gracious, instilling a sense of worth and value. An obligation, on the other hand, connotes insistence and a threat of failure.

Are there obligations in the Christian life? Of course. But unless those ought to's are framed with the overwhelmingly gracious invitation of God (which is already true for you), religious duty will suck the life from your desire to pray. God's relationship with his people is, metaphorically, a marriage commitment. What do we do first when we are planning a wedding? We draw up a list of people to invite. The invitation honors each of our chosen guests. Surrounded by cheering friends, we as a couple make vows—strong commitments—to one another as husband and wife. Over time many "have to's" are transformed into "want to's." Love grows, life bursts open, and joy floods our lives as we happily give ourselves away. Why is this the future of your praying heart?

Let's recall *perichoresis*. God, the three-in-one, is forever giving away his life to you. God's love floods you, his joy sustains you, his unity focuses you, and his glory directs you. God's forever conversation opens with a grand invitation: "Join in! Enter into the communicating life of the triune God."

You want to cry out "God, thank you, but I don't know how!" God reminds you of your heart transplant at the time of your salvation, that your new heart is already oriented toward and crying out to God the Father, through the Son, in the power of the Holy Spirit. The Father invites you to speak, and Jesus and the Holy Spirit are already and continuously praying for you. You jump in to this glorious God-conversation with passion.

God has given you divine vocabulary in the book of Psalms (and in other recorded prayers in the Bible, like Jonah's in Jonah 3). Just as he has provided air for your lungs to breathe, so he has gifted you with the psalms to facilitate your heart's ability to pray, sing, chant, or memorize. And once you begin enjoying the liberation of your praying heart through the praying of Bible prayers, you can experience any passage of Scripture as a starting block for a healthy prayer "run."

Madame Jeanne Guyon, a devout French woman of prayer who spent twenty-five years in confinement (prison) in the Bastille for her religious beliefs, wrote a treatise titled "Experiencing the Depths of Jesus Christ," in which she offered encouragement for those seeking to pray the Scripture: "To receive any deep, inward profit from the Scripture, you must read as I have described. Plunge into the very depths of the words you read until revelation, like a sweet aroma, breaks out upon you. I am quite sure that if you follow this course, little by little you will come to experience a very rich prayer that flows from your inward being."[47]

You might be thinking, "John, why didn't you just say at the beginning 'Learn to pray the psalms'? That would have saved a lot of time for you and us." It seems, actually, that I have come full circle to that simple direction: pray the psalms.

Yet if I had just written at the outset "pray the psalms," the outcome would have been deadly. You would have read, "I *have to* pray the psalms. I *need to* pray the psalms. I *ought to* pray the psalms." In a matter of days you would default to your vain repetitions and collapse into discouragement.

I have spent much time describing "what is" before we move on to "what may be." I want God's grand first move in the new covenant to be the compelling energy galvanizing your response. I want you to imagine yourself being swept into the eternal river of joyful, reciprocal communication with a vibrant, loving God. It is vital, however, that you never lose sight of this principle: in prayer, God is always first.

> The special place of the psalm in this "glorious course" is immediately obvious; for the psalm comes to being at the very instant when *the heart of the attentive believer*, having taken the Word of God, utters the word anew in the guise of prayer. This process occurs not at the level of the intellect but at *a far deeper level of the heart*, where we are able to listen to God and approach Him with the core of our personality[48] (emphasis added).

Very wise words, again, from Trappist monk Andrè Louf.

You may feel that I have been repetitive. If so, allow me to observe that you are perceptive. Repetition, after all, is the mother of all learning. I can't say enough about what God has already done for you. You are a praying person, meaning that you don't have to learn to pray. You now face the exhilarating process of liberating your already praying heart. In the next chapter I will offer simple incentives to spur you on as you chip away at the stone, setting free your praying heart.

# seven

## ABSORBING THE PSALMS

"Do not worry about the prayers you cannot pray. You yourself are a prayer to God at this moment," counsels O. Hallesby.[49] Indeed, you are a praying person. Your life itself is a prayer, for it is driven by a praying heart. Your challenge and mine is to bring this divine reality into our conscious thinking and verbal praying. We are invited to intentionally join in the grand conversation with God—the Father, the Son, and the Holy Spirit.

The primary reason so many people enjoy the writings of N. T. Wright is not so much that he is a diligent and well-respected New Testament scholar and historian but that he has kept himself close to the people by continuing to serve as Bishop in the Anglican Church. He is a scholar with a pastor's heart. Because of his scholarship, especially about Jesus in his first-century historical context, I have read many of his writings. I offer here a lengthy quote from his recent book *A Case for the Psalms*:

> The Psalms are among the oldest poems in the world, and they still rank with any poetry in any culture, ancient or modern, from anywhere in the world. They are full of power and passion, horrendous misery and unrestrained jubilation, tender sensi-

tivity and powerful hope. Anyone at all whose heart is open to new dimensions of human experience, anyone who loves good writing, anyone who wants a window into the bright lights and dark corners of the human soul—anyone open to the beautiful expression of a larger vision of reality should react to these poems like someone who hasn't had a good meal for a week or two. It's all here [in the psalms].[50]

## A SIMPLE SCHEDULE

In my early years of Christian growth I was encouraged to read five psalms and one chapter from Proverbs each day. In one month's time I did read all one-hundred-fifty psalms and all thirty-one chapters of Proverbs. I kept that schedule for many years—all the while with no awareness of the reality of my praying heart. Yet those were rich years of fellowship with God and growth in faith and wisdom. Eventually, as I became more "mature," I forsook that regimen, and my prayer life became more spontaneous and, sadly, more sporadic.

You might try that approach—five psalms per day for a month. If that seems too ambitious, read one psalm per day for five months. It isn't the amount that matters but the degree of attentiveness we bring to the Word.

The Spirit of God moved the psalmists to write so that their prayers (songs) would reflect the inspired Word of God. We speak our prayers as our own, and the Spirit and the Christ within us "resonate" with these "words of God." The words are addressed to God through us as part of the great circle of prayer. The God who listens is the God who speaks through you, making each of us an agent of God talking to God. Our praying heart sings and soars.

Why did Eugene Peterson translate the psalms into "street language" in his translation The Message? He explains:

> And so in my pastoral work of teaching people to pray, I started paraphrasing the Psalms into the rhythms and idiom of contemporary English. I wanted to provide men and women access to the immense range and terrific energies of prayer in the kind of language that is most immediate to them, which also

happens to be the language in which the psalm-prayers were first expressed and written by David and his successors. I continue to want to do that, convinced that only as we develop raw honesty and detailed thoroughness in our praying do we become whole, truly human in Jesus Christ, who also prayed the Psalms.[51]

Following is Peterson's creative translation of a Psalm 1:

How well God must like you—
   you don't hang out at Sin Saloon,
  you don't slink along Dead-End Road,
  you don't go to Smart-Mouth College.

Instead you thrill to God's Word,
   you chew on Scripture day and night.
You're a tree replanted in Eden,
    bearing fresh fruit every month,
Never dropping a leaf,
   always in blossom.
You're not at all like the wicked,
   who are mere windblown dust—
Without defense in court,
   unfit company for innocent people.
God charts the road you take.
The road *they* take is Skid Row.[52]

## BENEFITS

There can be no doubt that praying the psalms intentionally directs our heart toward God. Yet one of the benefits of doing so is that we intentionally connect with the "communion of the saints," past and present. We not only enter the joyful fellowship of Father, Son, and Spirit but are in communion with God's people throughout time and eternity. In terms of locality and solitude, we may be physically alone in prayer, but we are, indeed, joining an ongoing conversation that is both divine and human. We not only pray *in* the church; we begin to pray *with* the church.[53]

## WHOLE PRAYER

By "whole prayer" I mean that we are to bring all of our life—its countless intimacies and complexities, its darkness and light, its despair and joy, its love and hate—into the presence of God via prayer, and there is nothing in my opinion more conducive than the psalms to encourage this comprehensive approach. I've actually had people say to me after having prayed the psalms for a while, "I didn't know I could say that and say it *like that* to God." We've relegated prayer to the religious and holy rather than allowing it to be real and honest. We've sanitized prayer for our refined souls. "Don't give me any of that 'dashing the infants against the stones' stuff!" we want to say, shaking our heads as we read the imprecatory language in certain psalms. Indeed, some of us want to protect God from the sheer ugliness or stupidity of the human condition. Yet whether we like it or not, the psalmists "let it all hang out," so to speak. And speak they do.

Praying the psalms, then, thrusts us into whole prayer with the whole church, past and present. We become part of a colossal, almost unimaginable prayer meeting. As expressed by Gerald R. Wilson,

> Then, whenever you read the psalms, when you sing them or pray them, you are praying, singing, and reading alongside of a huge crowd of faithful witnesses throughout the ages. The words you speak have been spoken thousands—even millions—of times before: in Hebrew, Greek, Latin, English, and a myriad of other languages. As you read or sing or pray, off to your right stand Moses and Miriam, in front of you David and Solomon kneel down, to your left are Jesus, Peter and Paul, Priscilla and Aquila, while behind you come the voices of Jerome, St. Augustine, Theresa of Avila, Luther, Calvin, and more—so many more![54]

## HONESTY

Dishonesty in prayer devastates the soul. Using a quote from Isaiah the prophet, Jesus accused the religious leaders, "These people honor me with their lips, but their hearts are far from me" (Mark 7:6). Dishonesty. Hypocrisy. God is not fooled. We know this, but irrationally we forget it. Sin is irrational because it is born in idolatry. When we worship anything other than God in Jesus Christ, we are being irrational. Who made us, after all? Gives us breath, gives us life? Idols, either fashioned by humans or aspects of the natural creation, are anything other than our Creator. Pastor and spiritual director John Ortberg writes, "We all commit idolatry every day. It is the sin of the soul meeting its needs with anything that distances it from God."[55]

Immerse yourself in the psalms and you swim in an ocean of honesty, transparency, and gut-level frankness. "How long, O LORD? Will you forget me forever? How long will you hide your face from me?" (Psalm 13:1). Have you ever felt like that? Have you told God so? Or ask yourself whether David's rhetorical question from Psalm 139:21 resonates with you: "Do not I hate those who hate you, O LORD, and abhor those who rise up against you?" Whom, in fact, have you hated or perhaps hate even now (whether or not you know or suspect that person to be a God-hater)? Have you told God so?

God already knows our heart and thoughts, yet I believe he wants to hear us "say it"—for our own benefit. I'm reminded of God asking Adam "Where are you?" when we know God was not fooled by their hiding behind a tree in Eden, trembling in fear. Confession is so, so-o-o-o good for the soul. I'm reminded of my girls, years ago, playing in the living room with a blanket. They would cover up with it and cry out, "Daddy, come find us!" So I'd stalk around the living room, asking, "Are they behind the couch?" They would giggle under the blanket. "Are they hiding behind the bookshelf?" More giggling. "Where could they be?!" The girls would throw the blanket off and yell, "Here we are!"

That's what God wants from us. A hearty "Here we are!"

Many years ago when I was trying to wrap my arms around what holiness means in practical, day-to-day living, I wrote this down: *Honesty is a synonym for holiness*. You can't be holy and dishonest at the same time. If the psalmists guide us to anything in prayer, it is this: be honest before God. If you dislike somebody because they're bugging the daylights out of you, don't be sweet and syrupy in the presence of God when you talk to him about them. Just blurt it out: "I don't like John right now!" Honesty itself is a synonym for truth. The Spirit is magnetized to truth, to honesty, so much so that Jesus called the Holy Spirit the "Spirit of truth" (John 16:13). You are transformed in the atmosphere of truth by the Spirit of truth.

## DESPAIR

The twenty-five-cent term for this kind of psalm is *lament.* The psalms provide us a vehicle to give voice to our deepest hurts, disappointments, and dark side. We don't have to pretend that "every day with Jesus is better than the day before." Instead, we're invited to thoroughly speak our pain and despair to God. We can't avoid it, escape it, skim over it, or play it down but can only state it fully and bluntly. Walter Brueggemann, noting that pain often resolves into praise in the psalms, writes, "The praise has the power to transform the pain. But conversely, the present pain also *keeps the act of praise honest*"[56] (emphasis added).

My friend Dave teaches psychology and counseling classes at a local Bible university. Dave is in pursuit of helping the church at large learn how to lament. Many students sign up for his class to learn not just to become Christian counselors but to find healing for their own wounded lives. "The leaders of our churches have not taught the people how to lament; how to grieve the often deep and painful losses in their lives," Dave laments. We need this vital dimension of wisdom from the book of Psalms.

One of the most heart-breaking laments is Psalm 137. Written during the Babylonian exile, the psalm expresses the pain of the musicians who are forced to sing for sport, for the entertainment of their captors. The oppressors ask for "songs of joy" about Jerusalem, but these singers in exile cannot come through. "Every line of [Psalm 137] is alive with pain, whose intensity grows with each strophe [stanza] to the appalling climax."[57]

Psalm 137

By the rivers of Babylon we sat and wept
  when we remembered Zion.
There on the poplars
  we hung our harps,
for there our captors asked us for songs,
  our tormentors demanded songs of joy;
  they said, "Sing us one of the songs of Zion!"
How can we sing the songs of the LORD
  while in a foreign land?
If I forget you, Jerusalem,
  may my right hand forget its skill.
May my tongue cling to the roof of my mouth
  if I do not remember you,
  if I do not consider Jerusalem
  my highest joy.
Remember, LORD, what the Edomites did
  on the day Jerusalem fell.
"Tear it down," they cried,
  "tear it down to its foundations!"
Daughter Babylon, doomed to destruction,
  happy is the one who repays you
  according to what you have done to us.
Happy is the one who seizes your infants
  and dashes them against the rocks.

Appalling climax, for sure. We know that Jesus negated this kind of praying for his followers. The old "eye for eye, tooth for tooth" strategy was rendered obsolete by Jesus' teaching and example: "Father, forgive them for they don't know what they are doing." We may feel angry and want revenge, but that is no longer an option.

Contemptible speech is the most damaging to the soul. We read searing disdain at times in the words of the psalmists. When our highest expectations are shattered and our fondest dreams lie broken like scattered shards of pottery, we can easily move to contempt: to verbally attacking another's soul as though we are attacking their body with a sword. Contemptible speech is the seedbed for murder. Dallas Willard observes, "The intent and effect of contempt is always to exclude someone, push them away, leave them out and isolated. This explains why filth is so constantly invoked in expressing contempt and why contempt is so cruel, so serious. It breaks the social bond more severely than anger. Yet is may also be done with such refinement."[58]

Jesus does not want us to pray for vengeance with contempt coating our every word. In fact, he requires that we pray for the good of even our enemies: "You have heard it said, 'Love your neighbor and hate your enemy.' But I tell you: 'Love your enemies and pray for those who persecute you'" (Matthew 5:43–44). But *the feelings* of Psalm 137 are universal, real and relevant for our day in those times when our hopes are dashed or we have been abused, mocked, or taken advantage of. Don't forget: even this psalm was inspired by the Holy Spirit and is part of the Word of God.

When you encounter a psalm of lament as part of your scheduled reading at a time when your life is actually good and praise is coming easily, don't think of the words as inappropriate, meaningless, or misguided. Recall that when you pray something that doesn't "fit" you at the moment, God may apply your supplication to some other person or to thousands of others who are facing severe pain or distress. Not all of your psalm praying will be about you. As both Jesus and the Holy Spirit are interceding for you, you become an intercessor for others. On the other hand, on a day when you are down, hurt, or angry your scheduled psalm may be an expression of joyful praise to God, all happiness and light. Read it—and believe it. Somewhere someone else may be praying a lament for you, without even knowing you. The prayer world is huge! Infinitely bigger and better than the internet.

## THE A-B-C PSALMS

One of the most intriguing sets of psalms is called the "acrostic psalms." What is an acrostic? When I was the teaching pastor of Bella Vista Church in Rockford, Michigan, a one-of-a-kind lady (let's call her eccentric) would often hand me a note after the service. On it would be my name, J-O-H-N F-R-Y-E, followed by something like this: J-oyful - O-utgoing - H-onest - N-ice - F-aithful - R-eal - Y-oung - E-nthusiastic. That is an acrostic. I was glad my name wasn't Alexander Richard Stanfield. Connie used each letter of my name to write an attribute.

The psalms are works of literary art. They were not hastily conceived, off the cuff musings, but were written after deliberate thought and devoted meditation. The reason they touch us so deeply is that they were written so contemplatively. The acrostic poems (psalms) marvelously demonstrate this Hebrew artistic skill.

The psalms were originally written in the Hebrew language, and the Hebrew alphabet has twenty-two letters. An acrostic psalm uses lines of poetry, each starting with the next consecutive letter of the Hebrew alphabet. The mother of all acrostic psalms in Psalm 119. In this amazing psalm each letter is used several times in each section. Turn to Psalm 119, and note the Hebrew letter *aleph* just before the first eight verses. The next eight verses all begin with the second letter, *beth* (pronounced "bate"). All twenty-two letters of the Hebrew language are used to give full expression to the wonder and importance of the Torah, the Word of God. The psalmist wants to say all he can, from "A to Z," about the Law. Parenthetically, the other alphabetic acrostic psalms are Psalms 9–10, 25, 34, 37, 111, 112, and 145. The book of Lamentations[59] has three acrostic sections, and Proverbs 31:10–31 is alphabetically arranged.

Let me emphasize, not just the acrostic psalms but all of the psalms are poetic works of art. Thought, reflection, imagery, passion, and skill—all pulsate in this amazing book of prayers. There in your Bible you have at your ready disposal a depository of divine truth that *your praying heart longs to utter back to the living God*. Get on with it. Your prayer life will never be the same. Liberate your praying heart.

Meet Mary. She began the process of reading the psalms and discovered the liberating power of these ancient prayers. She absorbed the pastoral direction you have read in this book. I offered a series of sermons under the heading "iPray: Liberating Your Praying Heart." Afterward I asked Mary to share with you how she was moved to pray. Mary writes,

> Pastor John's sermon series "'iPray" made a very big impact on me. For me, learning to pray the Psalms was a whole new experience. John offered some good historical and theological insights, but setting those aside, I found the idea about already having a praying heart to be both deeply personal and very practical.
>
> The Psalmists were so open and honest before God. They expressed their emotions—fears, anger, bitterness and much more, openly before their Holy God. Their honesty amazed me. *I wanted that kind of relationship with my God.* I no longer wanted just words but real, honest conversations between myself and my God.
>
> I have chosen to embrace this "new" way of praying. Reading the Psalms daily and often; reading them out loud has become my "go-to" special place each day. My prayer life has not been the same since.

Mary has gotten in touch with, listened to, and joined her praying heart with the ongoing, loving, and transforming conversation among Father, Son, and Holy Spirit. God is tattooing his grace and love on her heart. Now it's your turn.

My hope has been that you will not feel pressured to pray because you've read this book. I have not tried to give you a four-step pattern or gimmicky scheme that might trick you into thinking prayer is easy. What I have tried my best to do is ground prayer not only in biblical truth but even more in the living, conversational interactions of Father, Son, and Holy Spirit. Let's briefly review those foundational realities.

## FOUNDATIONAL REALITIES FOR PRAYER

1. You are a praying person. This reality is grounded in the new covenant work of God in your life. The Spirit of God you received in salvation is an interceding Spirit. Three times in the New Testament he is referred to as "the Spirit of Jesus Christ"; know that

Jesus, too, ever lives to pray for you. Your new heart is oriented toward the Father, and the Spirit cries out in and through you, "*Abba*, Father."

2. Your praying heart longs to join into the joyful, unified, eternal conversation among Father, Son, and Holy Spirit. The supernatural dynamics of the *perichoresis* are available to you though Jesus Christ; note them in action in his great prayer in John 17.

3. Prayer, first and foremost, is initiated by God. The wonder of praying the psalms is that we enter into a dimension of "God praying to God." The psalms give us permission to bring our whole life, warts and all, before God. Even more, they offer us the vocabulary to do just that. And even more, as we pray the psalms we enter into a global act of intercessory prayer. As I was praying Psalms 6 through 10 this morning I was struck by the reality that I was mediating for the oppressed and marginalized of the world. Surely these psalms shaped Jesus' world-loving heart.

4. We all face hindrances to prayer, which I refer to as the stone around our praying hearts that must be chipped away. Your new heart knows how to pray—and it does, in fact, pray. We join in dialogue with God by cooperating with him to clear away the clutter; jackhammer away the stone; and free our joyful, passionate hearts for prayer.

5. The first and most profound result of praying is the deepening of your intimacy with Father, Son, and Holy Spirit. It is from that bonding—that "abiding," if you will— that the fruit of prayer begins to blossom and grow in your life. Prayer becomes a way of life—not a duty, Christian obligation, or spiritual discipline. Will it be difficult? Will it require change in you? Will it be challenged by the enemy and by your own slothfulness? Yes, yes, and yes. And yet, . . . yet, you will find that the indwelling Spirit of intercession and prayer will move powerfully to keep you before the Father and alive in Christ, the Son.

# eight
## NEVER SAY NEVER

Sitting in the quietness of a funeral home in Haslett, Michigan, listening to my friend and colleague Gary Raymond speaking the eulogy for his father, Harold Raymond, my praying heart cried out. I didn't know it at the time. It was January 1985. Gary was celebrating the many ways in which his father had influenced his life, and his tone was loving and joyful. As Gary continued the good words about his dad, I suddenly, without conscious intent, burst into a loud sob. I startled myself and my friend Don, sitting next to me. *What just happened?* I thought to myself. *Where did that come from?!* Somewhat embarrassed, I looked around to see whether I had disturbed anyone else.

Reflecting on that emotional outburst, I got in touch with a deep loss in my soul. I would never be able to speak good words about my father, as Gary had just done about his. As I shared earlier, my father had walked out of my life when I was ten years old. Only in my early forties did I get in touch with the huge reservoir of loss in my life as a result of having been abandoned by my father. My mother and father had divorced, and that sounds so benign and common. Yet this family-shattering reality was never explained to me in a way a ten-year-old could have understood. I lived for more than thirty years with no, none, zip, *nada* contact with my biological father. I had to make up my own reasons why he had left me—never good for a kid to have to do.

Thankfully, God brought into my life another man named Neal, whom my mother married about a year after the divorce. Neal has been a good influence on me and was a faithful husband to my mother for the rest of her life. Even with a stepfather, though, as I entered my late thirties I experienced a resurgence of curiosity about my "real" dad. *Where was he? What was he really like now?* Most of my impressions about my dad had been badly tainted by my mother's painful life with and memories of him. But I wanted to find out for myself.

During this time of questioning, some four years after the funeral of my friend's father, I was preaching a sermon series for my church titled "Finding the Father," based on Philip's request to Jesus, recorded in John 14:8: "Lord, show us the Father and that will be enough for us." Finding the Father is finding it all, was my premise. It is enough for us. I was weaving into the series my own search for my earthly father.

Through contact with my grandparents on my father's side, I found out that I had two half-sisters living in Florida. I called one of them—a surprise to her. "I'm trying to track down Dad," I said. "Oh, he lives just a block over from us," my half-sister responded, giving me his phone number.

On a Sunday afternoon I made phone contact with my dad. *What will my mom think of this when she finds out? I'm sure it won't be good*, I thought as I dialed his number. The phone rang and he picked it up.

"Dad, this is John," I said.

I don't remember all of that conversation. Our dialogue seemed strained and somewhat awkward. I do recall his commenting that it was good to hear from me. I responded that it was good to talk with him, too. Oh, and he said this: "I love you, son." *What?!*

I slammed down the phone in anger. Shocked and furious, I remember thinking incredulously, "You *love* me?! You *love me?* If that's the case, why did I have to call you after thirty years of abandonment?! You're the father. I'm the son. Why did I have to call you? What does 'love' mean to you, anyway?!"

A few weeks later I called my dad again. I had settled down and was more interested in initiating an ongoing relationship with him. We chatted superficially for a while. I told him a little about my life as a pastor, and he shared that he had been retired from the Navy for years. We agreed to keep in touch.

The church was interested in my journey to find my father, so I offered periodic updates on the search. One Sunday I reported that I had found my father and that he was living in Florida. I jokingly added, "If anyone's going to Florida soon, let me hitch a ride." After the service a good friend who flies corporate jets for a large furniture company approached me and announced, "I'm flying to Miami today. I'm taking some executives down who want to play some rounds of golf. We fly back Tuesday evening. I'll call you if there's room in the plane."

The phone rang. "John, there are actually two seats available. Does Julie want to come? Be at the airport at 4:00 p.m." I was stunned. Julie couldn't go because our youngest daughter was just a baby. But I was free to bring my oldest daughter, who was in junior high at the time. By 4:30 that Sunday afternoon my daughter and I were flying to Miami for free on a corporate jet!

We rented a car at the Miami airport, drove up the Atlantic coast, and spent the night in a hotel. By 9:30 the next morning we were pulling into the driveway of my half-sister's home. I was nervous. My half-sister was nervous. My daughter was just excited to meet her grandpa. My dad was nervous too. He was supposed to arrive at 10:00 a.m. No show at 10:00. Or at 10:30 or 11:00. "He's probably worried sick about meeting you after all these years," my half-sister put in. At close to noon Dad pulled into the driveway.

Only sixty-four years of age, he looked more like an eighty-four-year-old. He hadn't taken care of himself; a lifelong smoker and alcoholic who was now with his fourth wife, Dad was a mess, looking frail and bent at the shoulders, like a hawk. We shook hands and made quick introductions. Despite his dis-ease, Dad kicked into a jovial, everything-is-good persona. To allow my dad and me some time to catch up with one another—to shoot the breeze, as they say—my half-sister took her daughters and Leah to visit the nearby school. Awkward. How do you close a thirty-year gap in thirty minutes?

We tried. Dad remained superficial throughout the conversation, though I admit he knew a lot more about my life, family, and career than I had suspected. The family "grapevine" had been doing its job. I wanted to go deep quickly and ask, "Why in the Sam hill did you abandon me thirty years ago?!" but I knew this was neither the time nor the place for a confrontation. So we chit-chatted, both sensitive to the fragile nature of this initial reunion. Hopefully there would be additional opportunities to go deep enough to touch the pain and perhaps even heal some wounds.

Dad wanted to buy my daughter something from Ron Jon's Surf Shop, and for me he purchased a lottery ticket. Ironically, as we drove through town I noticed that the movie *Dad*, starring Jack Lemmon and Ted Danson, was playing at the local theater. It was November 1989. Upon arriving back at his home, my dad cooked a spaghetti dinner. We spent the night there, and after breakfast the next morning my daughter and I headed for Miami.

Dad died four months later; he suffered a massive brain aneurysm and was declared brain dead. My half-sister called to inform me that they were going to ask the doctors to "pull the plug" on Dad's life-support. I agreed. Dad was gone. And I was mad at God.

"All the days ordained for me were written in your book before one of them came to be" (Psalm 139:16). This verse infuriated me at the time. God is supposed to be all-wise, and all that he ordains is supposed to be the best and the wisest. So taught A. W. Tozer.[61]o *But how can living without my father for thirty years be wise, God? Tell me that! It's been hell for me. Then I go and make contact with him in the hopes of renewing our father-son relationship. Now he's dead. Thanks a lot, almighty, wise God!*

Julie and I drove to Jackson, Tennessee, where my Dad's funeral service and burial would take place. As we walked into the funeral home, the pastor of the church greeted us. This dark-suited, outgoing young man asked whether I was Wallace Frye's son. I told him who I was and that I was also a pastor.

Then it happened. The pastor told me, "I want you to come up on the platform with me and say a few words about your dad." Immediately I had a flashback to January 1985: *I will never get to say any words about my dad at his funeral.* Those were the words I had told myself back then as I grieved. Yet here I was, walking up to the pulpit in the Jackson funeral home to say a few words about how I loved my dad and had missed him all those years. Never say never to God.

It gets more amazing. The young pastor shared that my dad had come forward during an altar call in a revival service two years prior to his death. The pastor had asked my dad to meet him in his office the next day. No one expected my dad to show up, but he did. Dad reported regret over his empty and battered life. He was so empty that when he went to shave one morning he didn't see his face in the mirror. Just a hollow space. He agreed that his life was hollow; that image—or, as in the mirror, the lack of it—scared him. He wanted to get right with God.

My dad knelt on his knees in the pastor's office and prayed the sinner's prayer. He pleaded with Jesus to be his Savior. Imagine this: at his funeral service I learned that my dad had trusted Jesus as his only hope for freedom from a sinful life! Dad had told me nothing about this when I had met him four months earlier. I had sat there in that funeral home thinking, *I've complained bitterly to God how bad it was not having a dad around for thirty years, and now God is gently saying back, "Now you've got all eternity to spend with him."* Never say never.

My praying heart had prompted me to burst into tears at Harold Raymond's memorial service in Haslett, Michigan, in 1985. I know that now. My heart had cried out, *I want to bless my dad at his funeral.* My mind had concluded that this would never happen.

Since those days and those experiences I have been asking God to show me how I can cooperate with him in further liberating my praying heart. Like David in Psalm 27:8 ("My heart said, 'Seek his face.' Your face, LORD, I will seek"), I now am learning to discern the passionate cries of my praying heart. I want to be immersed in the eternal, joyful conversation among Father, Son, and Holy Spirit.

Your praying heart is real. It is passionate. And your new heart is heard by Father, Son, and Holy Spirit. Reverting once again to the vocabulary of David, we can do no better than to exult, "O LORD, our LORD, how majestic is your name in all the earth!" (Psalm 8:1).

# ACKNOWLEDGMENTS

The author gets his or her name on the book cover but don't be fooled by that. Every book is a team effort and this is a clear example. I want to express my appreciation to Tim Beals and the Credo House Publishers team. Tim has been an insightful and persistent encourager for this project. I thank Donna for her exceptional editing skill as she ironed out too many of my clunky sentences. I am indebted to Rick Devon, a friend and founder of Gray Matter Group for the book cover design. Two early readers were two of my (four) daughters, Elisha Francis and Shamar Collins. Their first affirmations helped me keep writing. I dedicate this book to my ten grandchildren in the hope they will continue the grand procession of pray-ers for generations to come. Another friend, Ginger Sisson, also offered strategic direction for the book. Many friends on occasion would ask me if I was writing anything and I would talk on and on about this project. For their patient listening and kind words, thank you. As always, I am thrilled that Rev. Canon Dr. Scot McKnight wrote the Foreword. His many books have informed and inspired me as I seek to live out the Jesus Creed. Scot is a respected New Testament scholar, yet I believe that what energizes his scholar's mind is a vibrant pastor's heart. Finally, yet importantly, I want to thank my wife, Julie. She cheered me on, often reminding me of the hard fact that the book would not write itself. Thanks, Julie, for your love and your prayers.

# ENDNOTES

1 Georges Bernanos, *Diary of a Country Priest: A Novel* (Cambridge, MA: Da Capo Press, 2002), 103, 104-105.

2 Gregory Boyle, *Tattoos on the Heart: The Power of Boundless Compassion* (New York, NY: Free Press, 2010), xiv.

3 Michelangelo, BrainyQuote.com, Xplore Inc., 2015. http:// www.brainyquote.com/quotes/quotes/m/michelange161309 .html, accessed March 26, 2015.

4 Eugene H. Peterson, *The Wisdom of Each Other: A Conversation Between Spiritual Friends* (Grand Rapids, MI: Zondervan Publishing House, 1998) 103.

5 Thanks to New Testament scholars like James D. G. Dunn, N. T. Wright, Scot X. McKnight, Kenneth Bailey, Larry Hurdado, and E. P. Sanders (along with many others), we know much more about the historical and cultural dynamics of the time in which Jesus and his disciples lived.

6 P. T. Forsyth, *The Soul of Prayer* (Vancouver, BC: Regent College Publishers, 2002 reprint), 34.

7 Josh Groban, "Broken Vow." https://www.youtube.com/ watch?v=Jo585KXHxO0 .

8 Joyce G. Baldwin, *Haggai, Zechariah, Malachi*. Tyndale Old Testament Commentary (London, England: InterVarsity Press, 1972), 190.

9 Richard Foster, *Prayer: Finding the Heart's True Home* (San Francisco, CA: Harper Collins, 1992), 133.

10 Andrè Louf, *Teach Us to Pray,* (Boston, MA: Crowley Publications, 1992), 10. Andrè Louf is a Trappist monk and a scholar of the Desert Fathers. His book is like high-octane fuel for firing up the praying heart.

11 A. W. Tozer, *The Knowledge of the Holy—The Attributes of God: Their Meaning in the Christian life* (New York, NY: Harper and Row, 1961), 9.

12 Tozer, 9.

13 Eugene H. Peterson, *Working the Angles: The Shape of Pastoral Integrity* (Grand Rapids, MI: Wm. B. Eerdmans, 1987), 32.

14 Peterson, *Working the Angles,* 37–39.

15 Peterson, 38.

16 C. Hassell Bullock, *An Introduction to the Old Testament Poetic Books* (Chicago, IL: Moody Press, 1979), 130.

17 "But there is reason for hope as well, since contemporary post-modernism looks much like the culture of the Graeco-Roman world into which the gospel first appeared some two thousand years ago." Gordon D. Fee, *Paul, the Spirit, and the People of God* (Peabody, MA: Hendrickson Publishers, 1996), xiii.

18 Dennis F. Kinlaw, *Let's Start with Jesus: A New Way of Doing Theology* (Grand Rapids, MI: Zondervan, 2005), 82–83.

19 Kinlaw, 28.

20 Justin S. Holcomb, *Know the Heretics* (Grand Rapids, MI: Zondervan, 2014), 90–91.

21 This view was called neo-Arianism after the heretic Arius.

22 Gordon D. Fee, *God's Empowering Presence: The Holy Spirit in the Letters of Paul* (Peabody, MA: Hendrickson Publishers, 1994), 101.

23 www.google.com/imgres?imgurl=https://frjamescoles.files.wordpress.com/2009/12/trinity-7661531.jpg .

24 www.uccyouthfrogsinc.2ofr.com/photo3.html .

25 N. T. Wright, *The Case for the Psalms: Why They Are Essential* (New York, NY: HarperOne, 2013). This book is a readable,

fascinating tour de force for reading, singing, and praying the psalms.

26 Kinlaw, 99.

27 Rebecca Konyndyk DeYoung, *Vainglory: The forgotten Vice* (Grand Rapids, MI: Wm. B. Eerdmans, 2014).

28 Leonard Verduin, *Somewhat Less than God: The Biblical View of Man* (Grand Rapids, MI: Wm. B. Eerdmans, 1970), 127.

29 Verduin, 117.

30 Henri J. M. Nouwen, *The Way of the Heart* (San Francisco, CA: Harper Collins, 1981), 45–46.

31 Peterson said this in a speech at a writers' conference at Spring Arbor College in 1987.

32 Eugene H. Peterson, *Answering God: The Psalms as Tools for Prayer* (San Francisco, CA: Harper Collins, 1989), 35–43.

33 Craig L. Bloomberg, *First Corinthians*, The NIV Application Commentary (Grand Rapids, MI: Zondervan, 1994), 164.

34 Peterson, 5.

35 Louf, 49–50.

36 Scot McKnight, *Praying with the Church: Following Jesus, Daily, Hourly, Today* (Brewster, MA: Paraclete Press, 2006), 53–54. Scot's book guides readers toward a healthy relationship between fixed prayers and personal prayers.

37 Wright, *The Case for the Psalms*, 22–23.

38 McKnight, 9–10. "We are invited to let our personal prayers be engulfed and enlarged by the prayers of the Church. We are invited to pray both in the church and with the church." 10. My hope is that this book will encourage that same experience for you.

39 http://www.michelangelomodels.com/m-models/how-he-made/how_he_worked_index.html .

40 Scot McKnight, *The Sermon on the Mount*. The Story of God Bible Commentary New Testament 21 (Grand Rapids, MI: Zondervan, 2013), 246.

41 Richard J. Foster and James Bryan Smith, Editors, "Revelations of Divine Love" by Julian of Norwich, from *Devotion Classics: Selected Readings for Individuals and Groups* (San

Francisco, CA: HarperCollins, 1993), 71.

42 *The Grand Rapids Press* (Michigan), April 28, 2001, A11.

43 McKnight, *Sermon on the Mount*, 247.

44 Dallas Willard, *The Divine Conspiracy: Rediscovering Our Hidden Life in God* (New York, NY: HarperCollins, 1997), 246.

45 Willard, 244–245.

46 Foster and Smith, "Life and Teachings" by Catherine of Genoa, 213.

47 Foster and Smith, "Experiencing the Depths of Jesus Christ" by Madame Jeanne Guyon, 321.

48 Louf, 51.

49 O. Hallesby, *Prayer* (Minneapolis, MN: Augsburg Fortress,1994 reprint), 150.

50 Wright, *The Case for the Psalms*, 2.

51 Eugene H. Peterson, "Introduction to Psalms," The Message: The Bible in Contemporary Language (Colorado Springs, CO: NavPress, 2002) 774.

52 Peterson, 775.

53 McKnight, *Praying with the Church*, 1–19.

54 Gerald R. Wilson, *Psalms Volume 1*, The NIV Application Commentary (Grand Rapids, MI: Zondervan, 2002), 14.

55 John Ortberg, *Soul Keeping: Caring for the Most Important Part of You* (Grand Rapids, MI: Zondervan, 2014), 83.

56 Walter Brueggemann, *Israel's Praise: Doxology Against Idolatry and Ideology* (Philadelphia, PA: Fortress Press, 1988), 139.

57 Derek Kidner, *Psalms 73–150*. Tyndale Old Testament Commentaries (London, England: InterVarsity Press, 1975), 459.

58 Willard, *Divine Conspiracy*, 152.

50 For a wonderful discussion of why Lamentations is a series of multiple acrostics, see Eugene H. Peterson, "The Pastoral Work of Pain-sharing: Lamentations," from *Five Smooth Stones for Pastoral Work* (Atlanta, GA: John Knox Press, p. 1975), 93–119.

60 Tozer, *Knowledge of the Holy*, 66.